GH00984179

Simply UK
Government Finances 2016/17

Foreword

Better information means better decisions

The public finances are always important, but they are even more critical today as we face the joint challenges of a slowing economy and pressures on public spending.

Understanding our government's financial position is essential if policy makers are to make informed choices about the future and if the general public is to properly hold the government to account.

That is why ICAEW is pleased to be able to support the publication of *Simply UK Government Finances 2016/17*.

Written by one of our members, who works with us on public policy matters, it shines a light into the opaque world of the public finances.

Simply UK will help everyone to understand the numbers that we hear about on the news (and many that we don't) and how they fit together to provide an overall picture of the government's financial position. It is also a powerful demonstration of the value a professional accountant can bring to the public debate on how the nation spends its money.

Improving transparency, accountability and financial management in the public sector all depend on the quality of the information available. And better information means better decisions.

Michael Izza
Chief Executive, ICAEW

Summary

The public finances remain fragile, but there is room for manoeuvre

The government's financial position is not strong.

Over the last decade more than £1tn has been added in debt, while other obligations have also grown significantly. Total liabilities now exceed £3.6tn.

Spending on pensions, welfare, health and social care all continue to be under strain from an increasingly long-lived population, while public services are also under significant pressure as spending is constrained by austerity.

Concerns about the level of future growth in the economy have been heightened by the uncertainty about the terms of our exit from the EU. This is particularly important given our continuing need to persuade financial markets to supply the around £140bn each year the government needs to be able to pay its bills.

Despite this, there are some positives.

The deficit has been brought down to the point that debt is no longer increasing faster than the economy. At the same time an extended period of low interest rates should keep interest charges low and provide some upside compared with the numbers in the 2016 Budget.

The government's decision to abandon its plan to eliminate the deficit within the next three years is also welcome. This allows some room for manoeuvre in supporting the economy, whether to relax austerity plans over the next three years, to defer planned tax rises or even to increase spending on the NHS.

Most importantly, there is now a real opportunity for the government to contribute directly to growth by increasing investment in infrastructure.

Martin Wheatcroft
Managing Director, Pendan

Contents

Start here

The numbers in *Simply UK* are primarily based on official plans or projections for the 2016/17 financial year included in the 2016 Budget published by the government. They have been updated for more recent financial information where possible. Projected amounts for the economy and population are derived from official statistics published by the Office for National Statistics.

Actual amounts may turn out to be different from the numbers shown here, especially for future years where there is more time for events, economic developments and changes in policy to have an impact.

Step charts

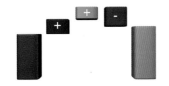

Simply UK uses step charts to bridge the changes between one year and the next. They can be confusing at first, but are really easy once you get the hang of them. The middle bars form 'steps' that indicate the changes between one year (the left hand bar) and the next (the right hand bar).

Just start with the amount shown in the left hand bar, then add or subtract each step to reach the amount represented by the right hand bar.

Key terms

2016/17	The financial year from 1 April 2016 to 31 March 2017
The government / the public sector	The UK Government, the Scottish, Welsh and Northern Ireland governments, local authorities, police & crime commissioners, public corporations and the organisations that they control (except for nationalised banks)
Tax	Taxes, duties, fees and other income of the public sector
Spending	Costs incurred by the public sector
Deficit	The shortfall when tax is less than spending
Surplus	The excess when tax is greater than spending
Debt	The cumulative borrowing of the public sector
GDP	Gross Domestic Product, an estimate of the total value of transactions generated within the UK economy
Inflation	The average increase in prices of goods and services across all sectors of the UK economy (officially the 'GDP deflator')
Economic growth	An increase in GDP after adjusting for inflation
An increase in economic activity	An increase in GDP per person after adjusting for inflation
National Accounts	The primary set of rules applied by the UK Government in preparing financial information and economic statistics
IFRS	*International Financial Reporting Standards*, a set of rules applied by businesses and many other organisations in preparing financial information†

For more information about terminology in this guide see page 76.   † See page 46 for the government's finances under IFRS.

Overview

Tax and spending

£56bn — Deficit

£716bn — Taxes and other income

Tax £716bn

£39bn — Interest on debt

£318bn — Public services

£175bn — Health and social care

£240bn — Pensions and welfare

Spending £772bn

Amounts are estimates per the 2016 Budget. Actual tax and spending may turn out to be different.

What should we all know?

Tax £716bn

The government expects to collect a total of £716bn in taxes and other income in 2016/17.

Planned tax and spending amounts are based on the 2016 Budget

Spending £772bn

The government plans to spend a total of £772bn in 2016/17, £56bn more than it expects to collect in tax.

Debt £1.6tn

Government debt is expected to increase from £1,602bn on 1 April 2016 to £1,638bn at 31 March 2017.

GDP £1.9tn

Gross Domestic Product (GDP), the estimated total value of transactions generated within the UK economy, is expected to total £1,943bn in 2016/17.

Population 65.8m

There are projected to be approximately 65.8 million people living in the UK as at 30 September 2016, the mid-point of the 2016/17 financial year.

How much is the government going to spend this year? How does that compare with the amount raised in tax? What is austerity and how is the deficit being reduced? How much is the national debt and what is happening to it? What is the size of the economy anyway?

The answers to these questions are especially important following the decision of the British people to leave the European Union.

Although some of the numbers in this guide are likely to change as the implications of the decision to leave the EU start to become clearer, it is important to realise that the big picture is unlikely to change significantly for the current year - there will still be a sizeable shortfall in tax compared with spending, and the government will continue to owe a sizeable amount of money.

And even as numbers change, *Simply UK* will provide you with a baseline for what is to come.

How will the now abandoned plan to eliminate the deficit by 2019/20 be amended following the decision to leave the EU? What will happen to our EU contributions? Will spending be increased or taxes reduced to stimulate the economy?

Simply UK will help you understand the key elements that make up the public finances and provide some insight into the economic constraints within which the government operates.

Numbers we might recognise

The government is really big

The UK is one of the biggest economies in the world and most numbers for its public finances run into the billions of pounds, or even the trillions. Their sheer size can be difficult to grasp.*

One way to understand what is going on is to work out each person's share of the numbers, by averaging the total amounts over the UK's population. For example, knowing that the government plans to spend an average of £185 per person per month this year on health is much easier to comprehend than the total spend of £145bn.

Caution is needed with per person numbers as even a small amount multiplied by 65.8m people turns into a very large sum of money.

It is also important to understand that averages don't provide a full picture of what is going on. Much more is contributed in taxes by those of working age for example, while children, low earners and pensioners typically consume more in benefits and services. Averages also do not take account of regional or other variations in tax or spending patterns.

For some items it may make sense to work out different averages than per person amounts. For example, the average cost of waste management of £10.50 per person per month on page 21 might be better understood as £25.20 per household per month. To avoid confusion only per person averages are presented in *Simply UK*, but for those wanting to work out per household averages just multiply per person amounts by 2.4.

Tax
£910 each
per month

The government expects to collect £910 per person per month in taxes and other income this year.

£1bn a year = £1.27 per person per month

Spending
£980 each
per month

The government plans to spend an average of £980 per person per month in 2016/17, £70 per person per month more than it expects to collect in tax.

Debt
£24,600
each

For each person living in the UK this year, their average share of government debt is expected to be £24,600.

GDP
£2,470 each
per month

Economic activity is expected to amount to an average of £2,470 per person per month for 2016/17.

People per
household
2.4

There are expected to be 65.8m people living in an estimated 27.4m households at 30 September 2016, an average of 2.4 people per household.

* £1tn = £1,000bn = £1,000,000m = £1,000,000,000,000 = £15,200 per person living in the UK.   £1bn per year = £83.3m per month = £1.27 per person per month.

Tax and spending per person

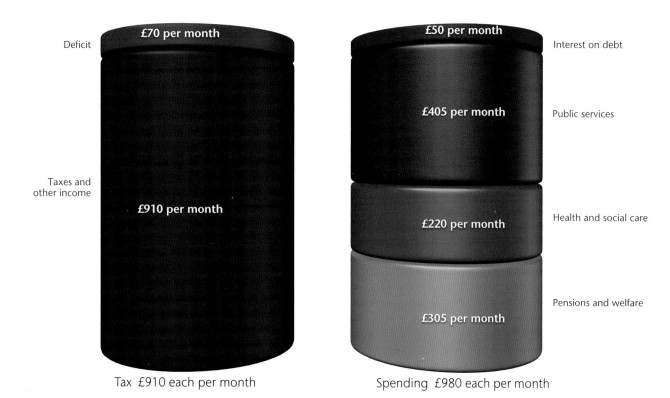

Deficit — £70 per month

Taxes and other income — £910 per month

£50 per month — Interest on debt

£405 per month — Public services

£220 per month — Health and social care

£305 per month — Pensions and welfare

Tax £910 each per month

Spending £980 each per month

* Based on a projected population of 65.8 million people living in the UK during the year and rounded to the nearest £5 per person per month.

9

Who collects and spends our money?

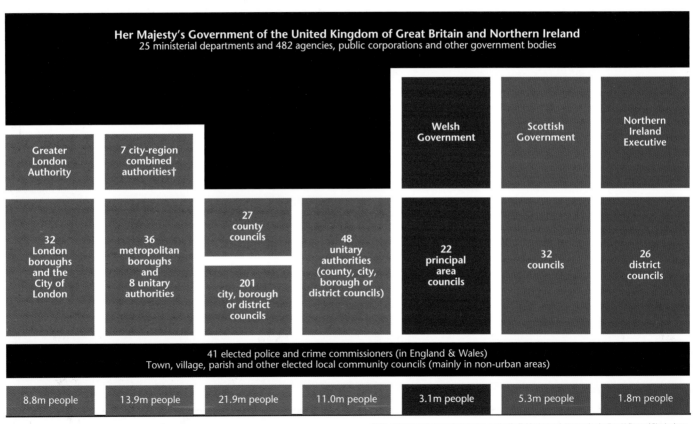

Her Majesty's Government of the United Kingdom of Great Britain and Northern Ireland
25 ministerial departments and 482 agencies, public corporations and other government bodies

Welsh Government

Scottish Government

Northern Ireland Executive

Greater London Authority

7 city-region combined authorities†

32 London boroughs and the City of London

36 metropolitan boroughs and 8 unitary authorities

27 county councils

201 city, borough or district councils

48 unitary authorities (county, city, borough or district councils)

22 principal area councils

32 councils

26 district councils

41 elected police and crime commissioners (in England & Wales)
Town, village, parish and other elected local community councils (mainly in non-urban areas)

8.8m people | 13.9m people | 21.9m people | 11.0m people | 3.1m people | 5.3m people | 1.8m people

† City-regions based around Manchester, Leeds, Sheffield, Liverpool, Newcastle, the Tees Valley and Birmingham.

Tax

How much is collected in taxes and other income?

The government expects to take in £716bn this year

At 36.9% of GDP, or almost three in every eight pounds generated by the economy, taxes and other income are expected to amount to £716bn this year. This is equivalent to an average of £910 per person per month.

The primary driver of the expected increase since last year is a projected 3.3% increase in the overall size of the economy, reflecting inflation of 1.5% and economic growth of 1.8%. Economic growth can further be analysed between a 0.8% increase in the population and an increase in economic activity per person of 1.0%.

The other main driver is a decision by the government to increase tax revenues. A number of new taxes have been enacted, existing taxes have been increased, and allowances and deductions restricted. There is also a major effort underway to reduce tax evasion and avoidance.

When combined with anticipated changes in the mix of economic activities (as different transactions are taxed at different rates), the result should be to produce an additional £16bn in taxes and other income on top of inflation and the growth in the economy.

Generally the forecasts for income in the Budget each year are reasonably accurate; for example last year taxes and other income came in £2bn (0.3%) lower than the prediction made in the 2015 Budget*. However, there is less confidence in this year's numbers given the heightened economic uncertainty following the UK's decision to leave the EU.

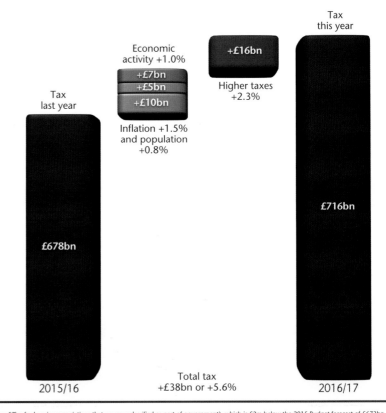

Tax last year

£678bn

2015/16

Economic activity +1.0%

+£7bn

+£5bn

+£10bn

Inflation +1.5% and population +0.8%

+£16bn

Higher taxes +2.3%

Tax this year

£716bn

2016/17

Total tax +£38bn or +5.6%

* In 2015/16 taxes and other income amounted to £671m (before including £7bn for housing associations that are now classified as part of government), which is £2m below the 2015 Budget forecast of £673bn.

What makes up taxes and other income of £716bn?

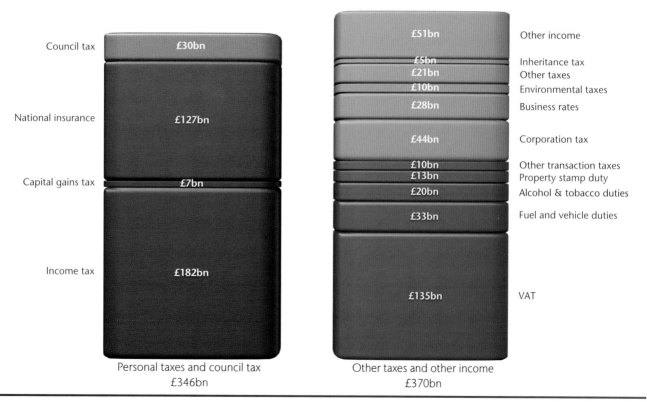

Council tax — £30bn

National insurance — £127bn

Capital gains tax — £7bn

Income tax — £182bn

Personal taxes and council tax
£346bn

£51bn — Other income

£5bn — Inheritance tax
£21bn — Other taxes
£10bn — Environmental taxes
£28bn — Business rates

£44bn — Corporation tax

£10bn — Other transaction taxes
£13bn — Property stamp duty
£20bn — Alcohol & tobacco duties

£33bn — Fuel and vehicle duties

£135bn — VAT

Other taxes and other income
£370bn

For more information about these taxes, see pages 68, 70 and 71.

13

Taxes and other income of £910 per person per month

Council tax — £38 per month

National insurance — £162 per month

Capital gains tax — £9 per month

Income tax — £231 per month

Personal taxes and council tax
£440 per month

£65 per month — Other income
£6 per month — Inheritance tax
£27 per month — Other taxes
£13 per month — Environmental taxes
£35 per month — Business rates

£56 per month — Corporation tax

£13 per month — Other transaction taxes
£17 per month — Property stamp duty
£25 per month — Alcohol & tobacco duties

£42 per month — Fuel and vehicle duties

£171 per month — VAT

Other taxes and other income
£470 per month

Amounts are based on dividing by a projected average population of 65.8 million people living in the UK during the year.

Spending

How much does our government spend?

The government plans to spend £772bn this year

Spending by both central and local government is expected to add up to £772bn in 2016/17. This is equivalent to around £980 per month for each person living in the UK, or 39.8% of GDP, just under two fifths of the overall economy.

Just over half (54%) of spending goes on what is sometimes described as 'the welfare state'. This comprises spending on pensions and welfare benefits, together with health services and social care provided to people living in the UK.

Most of the balance goes on public services provided by both central and local government, including education, defence, public order & safety, transport, housing and environment, industry, agriculture, employment and international development. There is also a further 5% that goes on interest charges on the national debt, benefiting at the moment from low interest rates and low inflation.

Spending is broken down further on pages 18 and 19, with average spending per person on pages 20 and 21.

It is important to understand that these amounts represent planned spending and that actual spending may be different. This year, interest on debt is likely come in under budget as interest rates remain very low, but this may be offset by increases in spending elsewhere.

Generally most governments have been able to keep to the planned total each year, finding savings in one area to offset overruns in another. For example last year's actual spending of £755bn was within £2bn (0.3%) of the amount originally predicted in the 2015 Budget.*

£39bn

5%
Interest on debt
£50 per person per month

£318bn

41%
Public services
£405 per person per month

£175bn

23%
Health and social care
£220 per person per month

£240bn

31%
Pensions and welfare
£305 per person per month

Spending £772bn
£980 per person per month

* The provisional outturn for 2015/16 (before including £11bn for housing associations that are now classified as government controlled) was £744bn, £2bn more than the £742bn anticipated in the 2015 Budget.

How does spending compare with last year?

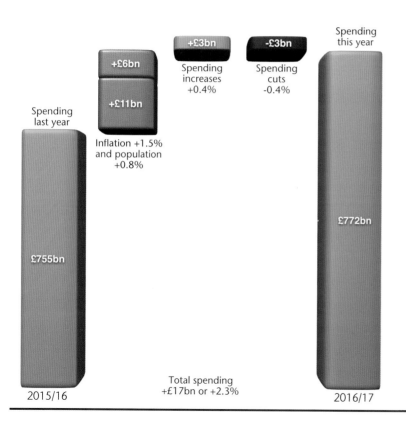

Spending last year

£755bn

2015/16

+£6bn

+£11bn

Inflation +1.5% and population +0.8%

+£3bn

Spending increases +0.4%

-£3bn

Spending cuts -0.4%

Total spending +£17bn or +2.3%

Spending this year

£772bn

2016/17

Some cuts, but overall a small increase in spending

Spending is expected to be £17bn more than last year, an increase of 2.3%.

However, once inflation and the increase in the number of people living in the UK is taken into account, spending per person is about the same as last year.

This may sound be surprising given all the discussion about cuts and the squeezes on public spending.

However, it is important to understand that there are significant pressures on spending from an increasingly older population, more to pay in interest as debt grows and political decisions to protect certain areas of spending, such as pensions, health and international development. There are also other pressures on spending, such as public sector pay and pensions, that mean that even holding spending still can be a significant achievement.

Areas of increase this year include health, where spending is expected to grow by £1bn in excess of inflation and population growth. Other protected areas include international development, where spending is also up by around £1bn. Combined with other spending increases adding up to around £1bn, this gives around £3bn of increases in total.

These are expected to be partially offset by cuts of £1bn to welfare benefits and £2bn in the cost of public services across both central and local government.

Where does £772bn of spending go?

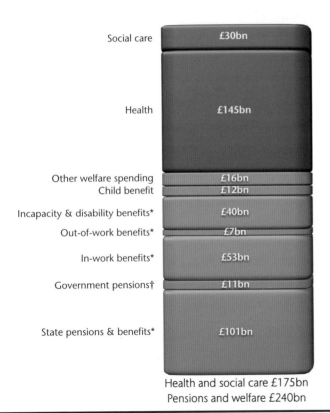

Social care — £30bn

Health — £145bn

Other welfare spending — £16bn
Child benefit — £12bn

Incapacity & disability benefits* — £40bn

Out-of-work benefits* — £7bn

In-work benefits* — £53bn

Government pensions† — £11bn

State pensions & benefits* — £101bn

Health and social care £175bn
Pensions and welfare £240bn

£39bn — Interest

£29bn — Other central and local spending

£20bn — International development*

£24bn — Industry, agriculture & employment

£29bn — Transport*

£34bn — Housing & environment*

£34bn — Public order & safety*

£46bn — Defence*

£102bn — Education*

Interest £39bn
Public services £318bn

* For a further breakdown of spending in these selected areas see page 19.   † A further £29bn for public sector pensions is funded from departmental budgets and current employee contributions.

Delving into detail

State pension & benefits £101bn		
State pension	£91.7bn
Pensioner tax credit	£5.8bn
Winter fuel allowance	£2.1bn
Free TV licences for over 75s	£0.7bn
Christmas bonus	£0.2bn

Public order & safety £34bn		
Policing	£18.5bn
Court services	£5.8bn
Prisons	£4.2bn
Fire services	£2.9bn
Border control	£1.1bn

In-work and out-of-work benefits £53bn & £7bn		
In-work tax credits & universal credit	£28.4bn
In-work housing benefit	£21.7bn
Maternity and paternity pay	£2.5bn
Jobseeker's allowance	£2.5bn
Jobseeker's housing benefit	£2.5bn
Income support	£2.4bn

Housing & environment £34bn		
Housing (inc. housing associations)	£15.6bn
Waste management	£8.3bn
Environment	£3.6bn
Community	£2.8bn
Water supply and street lighting	£1.7bn

Incapacity & disability benefits £40bn		
Disability allowances	£16.4bn
Incapacity benefits	£14.9bn
Attendance allowance	£5.5bn
Carer's allowance	£2.7bn
Industrial injuries benefit	£0.9bn

Transport £29bn		
Railways	£14.3bn
Roads	£9.6bn
Local transport	£2.8bn
Other transport	£2.1bn

Education £102bn		
Secondary schools	£39.2bn
Primary and pre-school	£31.7bn
Universities and higher education	£20.8bn
Training and other	£10.3bn

International development £20bn		
UK share of EU development	£6.8bn
UK share of EU external aid	£1.1bn
Direct international and humanitarian aid	£5.4bn
Policy, global and economic development	£4.0bn
Foreign office and other departments	£2.2bn

Defence £46bn		
Armed forces	£29.2bn
Support and equipment	£11.6bn
Security services	£2.6bn
Defence research	£2.0bn
Foreign military aid	£0.3bn

Other items of interest		
Cultural activities	£4.1bn
BBC and Channel 4	£4.0bn
Recreation and sport	£3.3bn
UK share of EU administration costs	£1.2bn
Royal Family	£0.04bn

Some of these numbers are estimated because the government does not provide an analysis of spending on a consistent basis between department budgets and the activities that money is spent on.

19

Spending of £980 per person per month

Social care — £35 per month

Health — £185 per month

Other welfare spending — £21 per month
Child benefit — £15 per month

Incapacity & disability benefits* — £51 per month

Out-of-work benefits* — £9 per month

In-work benefits* — £67 per month

Government pensions† — £14 per month

State pensions & benefits* — £128 per month

Health and social care £220 per month
Pensions and welfare £305 per month

£50 per month — Interest

£38 per month — Other central and local spending

£25 per month — International development*

£31 per month — Industry, agriculture & employment

£37 per month — Transport*

£43 per month — Housing & environment*

£43 per month — Public order & safety*

£58 per month — Defence*

£130 per month — Education*

Interest £50 per month
Public services £405 per month

* For a further breakdown of spending per person in these selected areas see page 21.   † A further £37 per person per month for public sector pensions is funded from departments and current employee contributions.

Delving into detail - per person

State pension & benefits £128 per month		
State pension	£116.50 per month	
Pensioner tax credit	£7.40 per month	
Winter fuel allowance	£2.70 per month	
Free TV licences	£0.90 per month	
Christmas bonus	£0.30 per month	

In-work and out-of-work benefits £67 & £9 per month

Tax credits & universal credit	£36.10 per month
Housing benefit	£27.60 per month
Maternity and paternity pay	£3.20 per month
Jobseeker's allowance	£3.20 per month
Housing benefit for jobseekers	£3.20 per month
Income support	£3.00 per month

Incapacity & disability £51 per month

Disability allowances	£20.80 per month
Incapacity benefits	£18.90 per month
Attendance allowance	£7.00 per month
Carer's allowance	£3.40 per month
Industrial injuries benefit	£1.10 per month

Education £130 per month

Secondary schools	£49.80 per month
Primary and pre-school	£40.30 per month
Universities and higher education	£26.40 per month
Training and other	£13.10 per month

Defence £58 per month

Armed forces	£37.10 per month
Support and equipment	£14.70 per month
Security services	£3.30 per month
Defence research	£2.50 per month
Foreign military aid	£0.40 per month

Public order & safety £43 per month

Policing	£23.50 per month
Court services	£7.40 per month
Prisons	£5.30 per month
Fire services	£3.70 per month
Border control	£1.40 per month

Housing & environment £43 per month

Housing	£19.80 per month
Waste management	£10.50 per month
Environment	£4.60 per month
Community	£3.60 per month
Water supply and street lighting	£2.20 per month

Transport £37 per month

Railways	£18.20 per month
Roads	£12.20 per month
Local transport	£3.60 per month
Other transport	£2.70 per month

International development £25 per month

UK share of EU development	£8.60 per month
UK share of EU external aid	£1.40 per month
Direct and humanitarian aid	£6.90 per month
Policy, global and economic	£5.10 per month
Foreign office and other	£2.80 per month

Other items of interest

Cultural activities	£5.20 per month
BBC and Channel 4	£5.10 per month
Recreation and sport	£4.20 per month
UK share of EU administration costs	£1.50 per month
Royal Family	5p per month

Some of these numbers are estimated because the government does not provide an analysis of spending on a consistent basis between department budgets and the activities that money is spent on.

21

How does spending vary by region?

From £885 per person per month in the South East of England up to £1,170 in Northern Ireland

Sending varies substantially by region and nation, but this is unsurprising given the differences between different parts of the UK.

For example, the southern half of England, with its larger cities and densely populated commuter belts, benefits from economies of scale in delivery of services as compared with Scotland, which has 32% of the UK's land but only 8% of the population.

Relative prosperity also affects the relative levels of spending, with a much lower level of welfare payments in the prosperous South East of England contributing to its lower level of spending than in other regions.

In England spending averages £740 per person per month, varying by region from £665 in the South East, £675 in the East of England, £695 in the East Midlands, £710 in the South West, £740 in the West Midlands and in Yorkshire, £785 in the North West, £800 in the North East to £840 in London.

These compare with the £845 per person per month in Wales, £885 in Scotland and £950 in Northern Ireland.

A further £220 per person per month needs to be added to the regional numbers for government spending that cannot be attributed to a specific region. This means total spending per person ranges from £885 per person in the South East of England up to £1,170 for Northern Ireland.

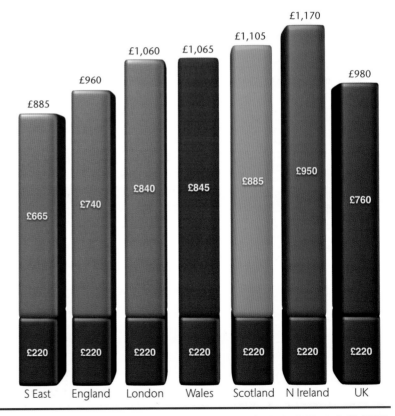

* Estimates based on data for 2014/15 extrapolated to 2016/17.

What does our money go on?

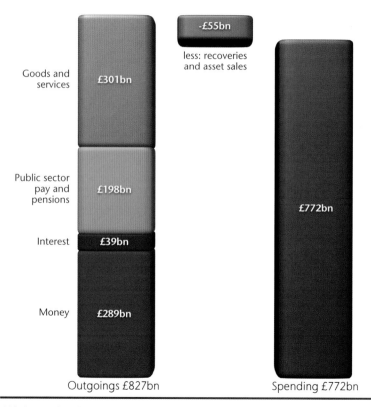

-£55bn	
less: recoveries and asset sales	

Goods and services — £301bn

Public sector pay and pensions — £198bn

Interest — £39bn

Money — £289bn

£772bn

Outgoings £827bn

Spending £772bn

Only a quarter of government spending goes on pay

Around 40% of total spending is in the form of giving money away, mostly without receiving anything in return. This is principally for pensions and welfare payments to individuals, but also for grants and subsidies, as well as for direct international aid and our net contributions to the EU.

After interest on debt, the balance of spending is in exchange for goods or services, including from employees.

Public sector pay and pensions make up around a quarter of total spending with 5.3m employees in central and local government to pay for. The average full-time salary is £34,000 per employee (not including pension payments to retired workers), while median pay is £25,000. There are 1.8m employees in health and social care, 1.5m in education, 0.6m in the civil service, agencies and public corporations, 0.6m in local government administration and 0.4m in the police and the armed forces

Goods and services are purchased principally from the private sector, but also from charities and other third sector organisations. These costs are partially offset by recoveries made by both central and local government for goods sold and services provided, as well as from asset sales.*

Recoveries are netted against the government's outgoings in this way in order to provide an indication of the net cost of providing services to the public. However, in doing so it obscures some spending and makes it harder to see how the numbers fit together. Similarly, by excluding these receipts from taxes and other income there is less clarity about how the government is managing its revenues.

* Other income and capital receipts (not including sales of financial investments) are expected to amount to £111bn in 2016/17, of which £56bn is included in taxes and other income and £55bn is deducted from spending.

23

How much of spending is on investment?

Investment spending of £83bn planned for 2016/17

Around 10% of total outgoings goes towards investment.

Of the £83bn planned for 2016/17, around £40bn is for economic and social infrastructure, with the balance going into military equipment, research and development and other forms of investment. The total includes £15bn in the form of capital grants, principally to universities and charities, but also to some businesses.

The government uses two measures for investment. The first is public sector gross investment. This is expected to be £78bn in 2016/17 and is net of £2bn from housing sales and £3bn from other asset disposals.

The other measure used is public sector net investment, which is expected to be £36bn this year. It is calculated by deducting depreciation charges on existing assets from public sector gross investment. This measure provides a proxy for 'new' investment going into the economy, as the government does not have a more accurate way of distinguishing between capital spending on new assets and that on replacing or renewing existing assets.

Transport investment includes £7bn on roads, £9bn on railways and £6bn on local public transport. Housing includes £7bn by housing associations, £3bn on existing and new social housing and £4bn on other publicly funded housing. Education includes £9bn on schools and £2bn in capital grants to universities and research institutions.

Universities are also the principal recipients of the £7bn incurred on research and development.

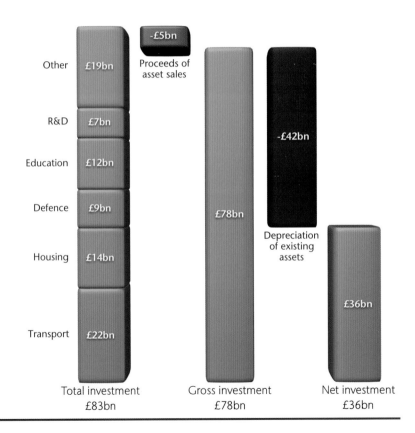

Deficit & austerity

What is the deficit?

A shortfall of £56bn this year

The deficit is the shortfall that occurs when taxes and other income are less than total spending.

This year taxes and other income are expected to be sufficient to pay for 93% of spending, leaving a 7% shortfall that needs to be funded by borrowing or selling assets.

Of course, borrowing to fund government expenditure is not unusual and many other countries run significant fiscal deficits as well.

However, the deficit here in the UK has averaged £100bn over the last decade, leading to the government borrowing in excess of £1tn in that time, a huge amount by any standard.

As shown on pages 29 and 30, the deficit peaked at £155bn in 2009/10, two years into the financial crisis. At 22% of spending, this was one of the highest deficits ever recorded.

Since then the annual deficit has been brought down through a combination of tax increases and austerity spending cuts. If achieved, this year's planned deficit of 7% of spending this year will be similar to levels last seen before the financial crisis.

The planned deficit for this year is subject to more uncertainty than usual, as priorities may change with a new Prime Minister and Chancellor of the Exchequer. Tax receipts may come in lower than expected depending on how the economy develops, although this this is likely to be offset at least in part by lower interest charges.

£56bn

Deficit
7% of spending this year

£716bn

Taxes and other income
93% of spending this year

£772bn

Spending

Tax

Spending

How is the deficit reducing this year?

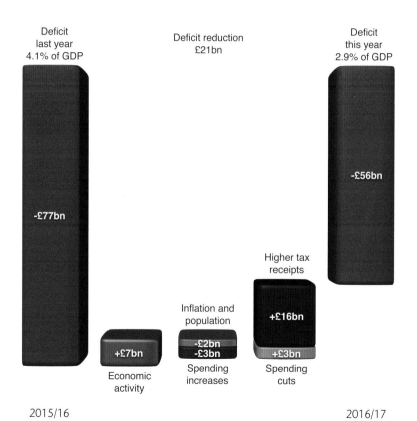

Deficit last year 4.1% of GDP

-£77bn

2015/16

Deficit reduction £21bn

+£7bn
Economic activity

Inflation and population
-£2bn
-£3bn
Spending increases

Higher tax receipts
+£16bn
+£3bn
Spending cuts

Deficit this year 2.9% of GDP

-£56bn

2016/17

Tax rises are the main driver of deficit reduction this year

The Budget 2016 plan is to reduce the deficit to £56bn this year, an overall improvement of £21bn compared with 2015/16. This is greater than the reduction of £15bn last year, when the deficit came down from £92bn in 2014/15 to £77bn in 2015/16.*

On a per person basis, the deficit is expected to reduce from approximately £100 per month in 2015/16 to around £70 per month this year.

Increased economic activity is expected to generate £7bn more in taxes and other income, but this should be mostly absorbed by a £2bn from inflation and a higher population, and from £3bn of spending increases in protected areas.

This leaves the main contributions to deficit reduction to come from £16bn in higher tax receipts and £3bn from spending cuts. This contrasts with last year when an increase in economic activity contributed £10bn and higher taxes contributed £7bn, while spending turned out to have increased by £2bn.

It is possible that the deficit may not reduce as expected, particularly in the light of the decision to leave the European Union. This could adversely affect economic growth, while the government might also choose to reduce taxes or increase spending in order to stimulate the economy.

If achieved, the planned reduction will take the deficit to below 3% of GDP for the first time since the financial crisis.

* 2014/15 deficit of £92bn (£655bn tax less £747bn spending) reduced by £15bn to £77bn in 2015/16 (£678bn less £755bn spending). 2016/17 deficit of £56bn is £716bn tax less £772bn spending.

27

Assessing the deficit

Really bad, a bit bad or possibly even good?

Deciding whether and when running a deficit is good or bad idea is a matter of extensive debate amongst both economists and politicians.

After all, most governments in developed countries choose to run a deficit, using borrowing to fund a proportion of their spending.

One view is that all deficits are bad, in which case this year's deficit is 'bad' by £56bn.

A common view, however, is that the bad element is the structural deficit: borrowing that adds permanently to the national debt. It is calculated by excluding borrowing in the lower half of the economic cycle that should in theory be repaid at the top. This cyclical borrowing is estimated at £2bn out of the £56bn expected deficit this year.

Another approach is to differentiate the deficit between borrowing used to fund current government spending and that used to fund new investment. Borrowing to invest may make sense if it generates future economic growth, while borrowing to fund current spending is looked on less favourably.

A third method is based on looking at whether the deficit is causing the national debt to increase or fall as a proportion of GDP. In theory the deficit could be as high as £71bn and debt would still be 'inflated away' by the expected increase in GDP this year. As a consequence, the deficit could be £15bn higher and still be good from this perspective, subject to the economy growing in line with expectations.

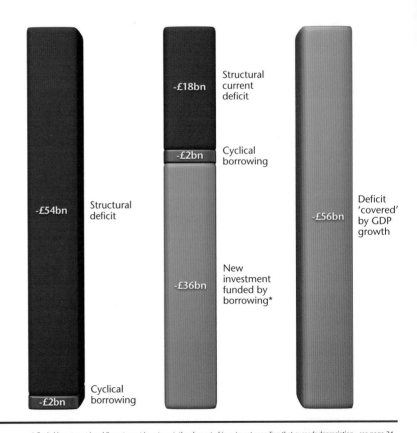

-£54bn — Structural deficit

-£2bn — Cyclical borrowing

-£18bn — Structural current deficit

-£2bn — Cyclical borrowing

-£36bn — New investment funded by borrowing*

-£56bn — Deficit 'covered' by GDP growth

* Capital investment is public sector net investment, the element of investment spending that exceeds depreciation - see page 24.

A decade of deficits

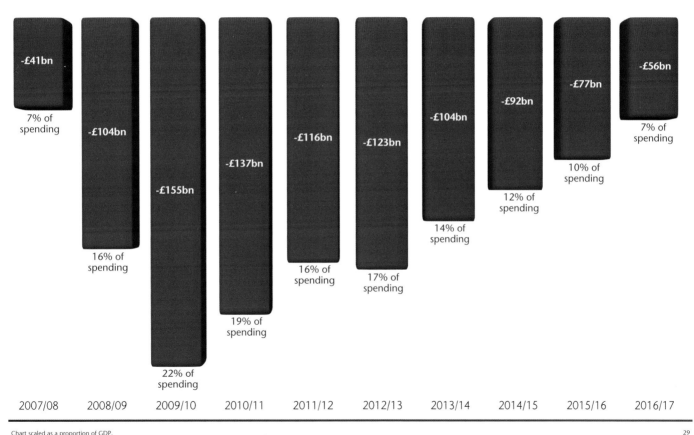

-£41bn
7% of spending

-£104bn
16% of spending

-£155bn
22% of spending

-£137bn
19% of spending

-£116bn
16% of spending

-£123bn
17% of spending

-£104bn
14% of spending

-£92bn
12% of spending

-£77bn
10% of spending

-£56bn
7% of spending

2007/08   2008/09   2009/10   2010/11   2011/12   2012/13   2013/14   2014/15   2015/16   2016/17

Chart scaled as a proportion of GDP.

Deficit reduction to date

Austerity spending cuts have made the biggest contribution to reducing the deficit so far

The deficit has reduced substantially since the financial crisis, down from its peak of £155bn in 2009/10 to an expected £56bn this year, a £99bn a year improvement.*

Of this the economy contributed £55bn, but this was absorbed by £20bn from the effects of inflation and population growth and by £38bn of spending increases in protected areas, such as pensions, interest, health and international development.

As a consequence the main contributors to deficit reduction have been from increases in taxes and other income of £22bn and from cuts in annual spending of £80bn.

Unfortunately, the economy has grown more slowly than was hoped for back in 2010, with taxes and other income around £50bn a year below the forecasts from that time.

It is difficult to know what might have happened if austerity had not been implemented, or had it been less severe. Some economists and politicians argue that the austerity programme of spending cuts are the primary reason that economic growth has been less strong than hoped for over the last seven years.

Others believe that it would have been difficult to persuade investors to lend the government the very large sums it has needed to pay its bills if there had not been a plan to reduce spending significantly.

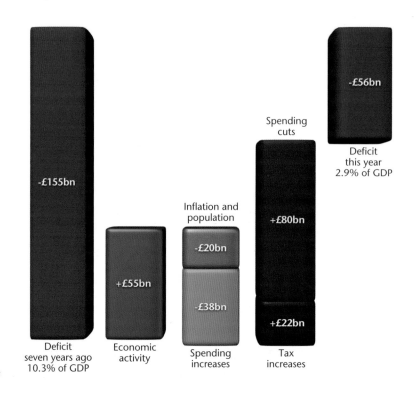

-£155bn	Deficit seven years ago 10.3% of GDP
+£55bn	Economic activity
-£20bn / -£38bn	Inflation and population / Spending increases
+£80bn / +£22bn	Spending cuts / Tax increases
-£56bn	Deficit this year 2.9% of GDP

2009/10

2016/17

* Comparison between taxes and other income of £538bn and spending of £693bn in 2009/10 with taxes and other income of £716bn and spending of £772bn in 2016/17.

Austerity: £80bn of cuts offset by £38bn of increases in protected areas

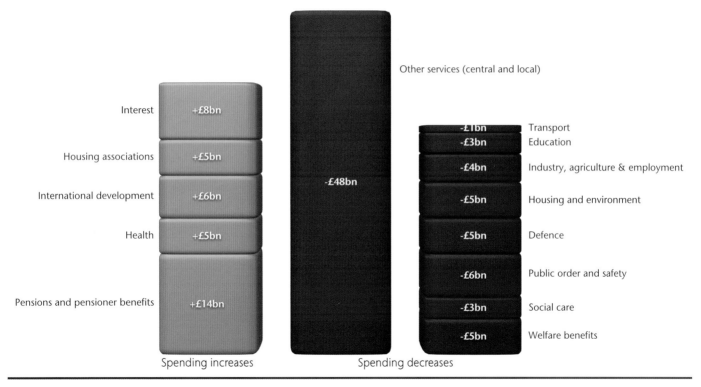

Spending increases:
- Interest +£8bn
- Housing associations +£5bn
- International development +£6bn
- Health +£5bn
- Pensions and pensioner benefits +£14bn

Spending decreases:
- Other services (central and local) -£48bn
- Transport -£1bn
- Education -£3bn
- Industry, agriculture & employment -£4bn
- Housing and environment -£5bn
- Defence -£5bn
- Public order and safety -£6bn
- Social care -£3bn
- Welfare benefits -£5bn

Changes in annual spending between 2009/10 and 2015/16, after adjusting for inflation and population growth.

31

What is the plan for the deficit in the future?

The (abandoned) fiscal charter

The government is required by law to adopt a fiscal charter setting out how it plans to manage its finances over the medium term.

The current fiscal charter was approved by Parliament in 2015 and commits the government to completely eliminating the deficit by 2019/20.

The 2016 Budget included a plan to achieve this, based on the economy continuing to recover (producing higher tax revenues), combined with tax rises and further spending cuts. If achieved it would result in tax exceeding spending in 2019/20 to generate a £10bn surplus.

However, the government has announced that in the light of the decision to leave the EU it has now abandoned the goal of a balanced budget within the next three years. It will instead adopt a longer timescale to eliminate the deficit.

This decision was partly because of concerns that economic growth will not be as strong as expected. Keeping to the announced target of a balanced budget might then require actions such as additional austerity or tax increases in order to make up for lost tax revenue. This could adversely affect the economy just at the time it needs a boost.

Adopting a new fiscal charter with a more relaxed timescale for eliminating the deficit will provide some flexibility to the government to reduce taxes or increase spending in order to provide more stimulus to the economy, potentially including more investment in infrastructure to support future economic growth.

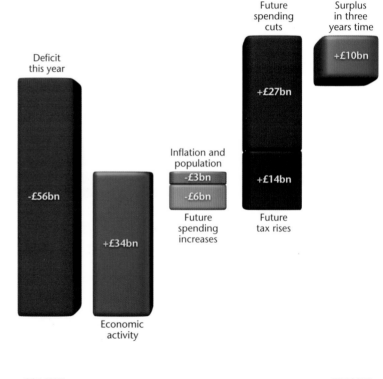

Comparison between forecast tax of £673bn and planned spending of £742bn in 2015/16 and projected tax and spending of £814bn and £804bn respectively in 2019/20.

Debt

How much do we owe (and to whom)?

Average net debt of £1,620,000,000,000, equivalent to £24,600 for each person in the UK

The largest element of debt is in the form of British Government bonds traded on the London Stock Exchange. Known as gilts, these are issued in two varieties: fixed-interest and index-linked, the latter principally linked to the retail prices index. This is followed by borrowing directly from the public through National Savings premium bonds and savings certificates. Other amounts owed include the external debts of local authorities, short-term Treasury bills, bank loans, foreign currency loans and the debt of publicly owned corporations. These are partially offset by cash balances and other financial assets.

Contrary to common belief, the majority of the nation's debt is not owed to overseas investors; instead the majority of debt is owed to domestic UK investors, with overseas holdings of around a quarter of the total.

One of the largest holders of gilts is the Bank of England, an institution owned by the government, which has £375bn invested in gilts from 'quantitative easing' transactions used to support the financial system. It is important to realise that the Bank of England financed the majority of these purchases by increasing the amounts that it owes to UK banks. Hence the government still has a debt obligation, just in a different form. One benefit is the around £12bn in interest a year that it keeps from the difference between the interest on the gilts it owns and the almost zero interest payable to the banks holding Bank of England deposits.

Debt is only one part of the government's total liabilities. More information about its other liabilities is on page 50.

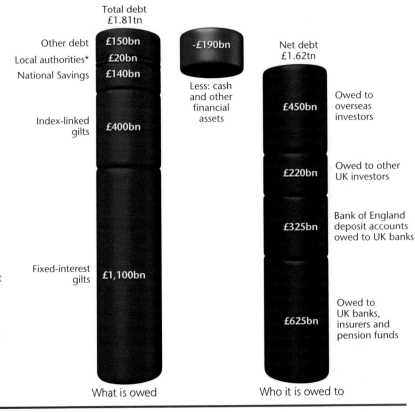

Total debt
£1.81tn

Other debt	£150bn
Local authorities*	£20bn
National Savings	£140bn
Index-linked gilts	£400bn
Fixed-interest gilts	£1,100bn

What is owed

-£190bn

Less: cash and other financial assets

Net debt
£1.62tn

£450bn — Owed to overseas investors

£220bn — Owed to other UK investors

£325bn — Bank of England deposit accounts owed to UK banks

£625bn — Owed to UK banks, insurers and pension funds

Who it is owed to

Debt shown is based on an estimate of the average amount of debt during 2016/17.   * Local authorities total debt is around £90bn, but of this £70bn os owed to central government and is offset in these numbers.

Is debt going up or down?

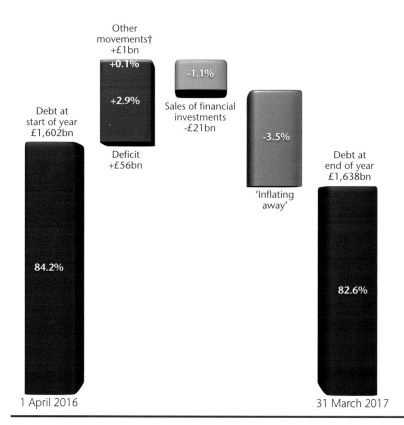

Other movements†
+£1bn
+0.1%

+2.9%

Debt at start of year
£1,602bn

Deficit
+£56bn

-1.1%

Sales of financial investments
-£21bn

-3.5%

'Inflating away'

Debt at end of year
£1,638bn

84.2%

82.6%

1 April 2016

31 March 2017

Debt continues to increase, but it is starting to fall as a share of GDP

Although borrowing to fund the deficit will result in more debt, the government will instead tell you that debt is falling.

This is because its preferred approach is to measure debt in terms of how it compares with the the size of the economy. If GDP increases, then debt as a share of GDP will decrease.

This effect is sometimes described as 'inflating away' the debt and conceptually is similar to the way your mortgage becomes more affordable when your salary goes up.

Unfortunately this is not the most reliable of performance measures as both debt and GDP can change significantly depending on the health of the economy and other changes in circumstances.

This was illustrated by the coalition government's announcement in March 2015 that debt would start to fall in 2015/16. Several revisions later to both the way debt and GDP are calculated, together with slightly higher borrowing and slightly lower economic growth, means that debt as a share of GDP is now reported to have increased by 1.0% from 83.2% to 84.2% last year instead of the originally predicted decrease of 0.2% from 80.4% to 80.2%.

As a consequence, some caution should be expressed as to the projected fall in debt as a share of GDP shown here, especially as sales of financial investments are likely to be less than predicted, while economic uncertainty may affect both GDP and the deficit.

A decade of increasing debt

Total borrowing
over ten years
£1,109bn

| +6% |
| +3% |
| +4% |
| +5% |
| +6% |
| +7% |
| +7% |
| +9% |
| +10% |
| +7% |
| +3% |

Other*:	£104bn
2016/17:	£56bn
2015/16:	£77bn
2014/15:	£92bn
2013/14:	£104bn
2012/13:	£123bn
2011/12:	£116bn
2010/11:	£137bn
2009/10:	£155bn
2008/09:	£104bn
2007/08:	£41bn

-19%

Reduction in debt as
a proportion of GDP
because of inflation
and economic growth

National debt
at the end of this year
£1,638bn

83%

National debt
ten years ago
£529bn

35%

31 Mar 2007

31 Mar 2017

* Other relates to the purchase and sale of financial investments (primarily from bank nationalisations) and to cash flow timing, exchange movements and Bank of England financial operations.

How much do we need to borrow this year?

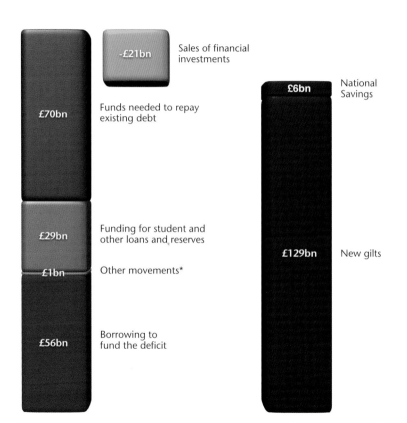

-£21bn — Sales of financial investments

£70bn — Funds needed to repay existing debt

£29bn — Funding for student and other loans and reserves

£1bn — Other movements*

£56bn — Borrowing to fund the deficit

£6bn — National Savings

£129bn — New gilts

Total borrowing is expected to be £135bn in 2016/17

Total planned borrowing for this year is actually much greater than the headline deficit of £56bn, even though there are £21bn in planned sales of financial investments to take into account.

This is principally because £70bn is needed to repay existing debt that falls due during the year.

In addition, £29bn is needed to fund student and other loans and reserves. This includes £15bn in student loans, £7bn in other loans (including 'Help To Buy' loans for first time homebuyers, the Green Investment Bank, the British Business Bank, and loans to international aid programmes), together with £6bn to fund an increase in the government's foreign currency reserves and a net £1bn in other funding requirements.

As a consequence, the government needs to borrow a total of £135bn this year. Most of this will come from issuing £129bn in new gilts to banks and other investors through the London Stock Exchange, leaving £6bn to be raised directly from the public through National Savings.

The total amount borrowed this year will be affected by the overall economy and hence the final totals for taxes and other income and for spending. It will also be affected by the proceeds from the sale of financial investments, which are likely to be less than anticipated because of a fall in the value of the £9bn in Lloyds Bank and RBS shares expected to be sold this year. Some of these sales are being postponed to future years, increasing the amount that will need to be borrowed by the government this year.

* Other movements in debt arise from cash timing differences, exchange movements and financial operations.

Financing over the next five years

A borrowing requirement of £140bn or so a year

Although the 2016 Budget indicates that the deficit is expected to turn into a a surplus by 2019/20, the amount we need to borrow is not expected to fall at the same rate.

This is primarily because, as set out on the previous page, the government needs to borrow substantial sums of money to repay existing debt as it falls due, as well as needing to fund student and other loans and reserves.

As a consequence, the government expects to have to raise somewhere in the order of £700bn from the financial markets over the next five years, even though net debt is expected to increase by 'only' £138bn over that that time.

One positive development is that the team responsible for managing the national debt, the Debt Management Office, has increased the average maturity of government debt to approximately 16 years, with the longest gilt in issue not due for repayment until 2068.

By borrowing over longer periods, the amount of debt that will need to be refinanced will fall from 2021 onwards, while the government is also able to 'lock in' low interest rates for longer.

The need to raise so much money each year means that the government is reliant on the financial markets continuing to have confidence in the long-term economic viability of the UK. Continuing that confidence will be particularly important as a new structure for the UK economy is developed as we depart from the European Union.

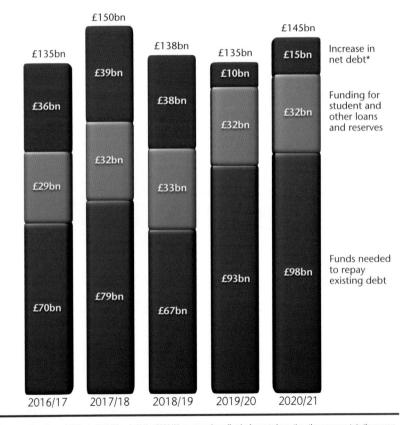

* Increase in net debt = deficit (or surplus) less asset sales and other movements. The expected surpluses of £10bn in 2019/20 and £11bn 2020/21 are more than offset by forecasted negative other movements in those years.

European Union

How much goes to the EU?

The EU costs the UK about £8bn a year, or around £10 per person per month

This is less than our headline membership fee, which this year is estimated to be £15.1bn (£290m a week or £19 per person per month). Our gross contribution is calculated based on the size of the UK economy, together with a share of VAT revenues, and three-quarters of import duties on goods imported from outside the EU, less a special rebate agreed with other European countries.

Some £6.0bn of the money we pay to the EU is then sent back to us. This includes £3.3bn in agricultural subsidies and rural development, £1.2bn in regional and social development funding and £1.5bn in other spending on EU programmes in the UK, including grants to British universities and research institutions. In addition, our fee includes £1.1bn in international aid that goes outside the EU and is funded out of the UK's international development budget.

As a consequence, the net cost to the UK of being a member is closer to £8.0bn a year, equivalent to around £155m a week or £10 per person per month.

Of this amount approximately £1.2bn (£23m a week or £1.50 per person per month) goes towards the running costs of the EU. This is 0.2% of total government spending.

The balance of £6.8bn (£132m a week or £8.60 per person per month) goes towards regional and social development funding for poorer countries in the EU, in particular to the eastern European countries that have joined the EU since the collapse of communism.

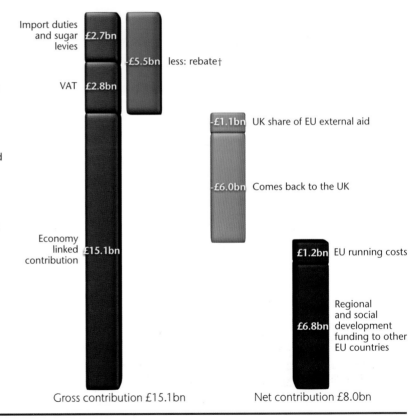

Import duties and sugar levies £2.7bn

£5.5bn less: rebate†

VAT £2.8bn

-£1.1bn UK share of EU external aid

-£6.0bn Comes back to the UK

Economy linked contribution £15.1bn

£1.2bn EU running costs

£6.8bn Regional and social development funding to other EU countries

Gross contribution £15.1bn

Net contribution £8.0bn

† It is coincidence that the rebate this year equals the total of VAT and custom duties and sugar levies. It is different in other years.

How big is the EU budget?

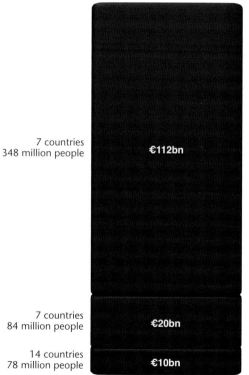

7 countries 348 million people	€112bn
7 countries 84 million people	€20bn
14 countries 78 million people	€10bn

2016 contributions

Germany	€30.1bn
France	€21.8bn
UK†	€19.8bn
Italy	€15.9bn
Spain	€11.3bn
Netherlands	€8.0bn
Belgium	€5.5bn
Poland	€4.5bn
Sweden	€4.4bn
Austria	€3.1bn
Denmark	€2.8bn
Finland	€2.0bn
Greece	€1.8bn
Ireland	€1.8bn
Portugal	€1.7bn
Romania	€1.6bn
Czech Republic	€1.6bn
Hungary	€1.1bn
Slovakia	€0.8bn
Bulgaria	€0.4bn
Croatia	€0.4bn
Slovenia	€0.4bn
Lithuania	€0.4bn
Luxembourg	€0.3bn
Latvia	€0.3bn
Estonia	€0.2bn
Cyprus	€0.2bn
Malta	€0.1bn

A budget of €142bn for 2016

The European Union's total budget for 2016 of €142bn is paid for by contributions from its member countries, including the UK. Contributions are linked to the size of the economies of each country, with the largest and wealthiest countries contributing the most.

The UK's contribution is less than the size of its economy would imply because of a rebate that reduces its contribution. The majority of the rebate is funded by France, Italy and Spain, reflecting their greater benefit from agricultural subsidies.

With an estimated population of 510 million people in 2016, EU contributions are equivalent to an average of around €23 per person per month.

Contributions range from €5 per person per month for Bulgaria up to €45 per person per month for Luxembourg, as shown on page 43.

The UK gross contribution is €25 per person per month (net of rebate). This was around £19 per month once converted into sterling (see page 40).

The official EU Budget excludes contributions and spending by the European Economic Area countries (Norway, Iceland and Liechtenstein) of around €1bn a year in total. Norway contributes almost all of that amount, equivalent to a contribution of approximately €14 per person per month by the Norwegian people.

---

† The UK contribution shown is net of its rebate.

Where does the money go?

Most EU spending goes into regional and social development or on agricultural support

The largest development programmes are the European Regional Development Fund (€29bn), the Cohesion Fund (€7bn) and the European Social Fund (€12bn).

Regional and social development includes €10bn in aid to countries outside the EU, including EU candidate countries.

Agricultural support comprises €39bn in farming subsidies, €3bn for intervening in agricultural markets and €1bn supporting fishing and maritime industries, complemented by rural development spending amounting to around €12bn.

EU programmes cover a wide range of activities and projects, including €3bn for education and culture and €3bn on security and justice cooperation.

There is also €2bn for satellite and space programmes and over €2bn on research and development.

The budget for administration of €9bn includes the €4bn cost of running the European Commission and other central bodies. Around €2bn goes on the combined cost of its governing institutions, the EU Council and the EU Parliament, while around €2bn is spent on administering programmes.

EU institutions — €9bn

EU programmes — €22bn

Agricultural support and rural development — €55bn

Regional and social development — €58bn

Net expenditure €142bn

* Net expenditure is after deducting €2bn in income generated directly by EU institutions, reducing the net cost to EU member states.

EU average gross contribution of €23 per person per month

Average contribution per person

€23 per month

Contributions

Belgium	€40 per month
Netherlands	€39 per month
Germany	€31 per month
France	€27 per month
UK†	€25 per month
Italy	€22 per month
Spain	€20 per month
Denmark	€41 per month
Sweden	€37 per month
Ireland	€32 per month
Austria	€30 per month
Finland	€30 per month
Greece	€14 per month
Poland	€10 per month
Luxembourg	€45 per month
Slovenia	€17 per month
Malta	€17 per month
Cyprus	€16 per month
Estonia	€14 per month
Portugal	€14 per month
Czech Republic	€13 per month
Slovakia	€12 per month
Lithuania	€12 per month
Latvia	€11 per month
Hungary	€9 per month
Croatia	€9 per month
Romania	€7 per month
Bulgaria	€5 per month

€1 per month — EU institutions

€4 per month — EU programmes

€9 per month — Agricultural support and rural development

€9 per month — Regional and social development

Expenditure

What next for our EU contributions?

Will we continue to support eastern Europe?

One major element of the negotiation to leave the EU will concern money.

Part of the EU budget for the UK is on the basis that the UK receives back what it puts in. Hence there should in theory be no significant financial impact from exiting the EU in those areas, as most of this spending will revert to being a UK responsibility. Agricultural subsidies and regional and social development in the UK are examples. In addition, international aid that is currently channelled through the EU will still be incurred if it reverts back to the UK.

We are likely to want to continue to participate in some EU programmes, for example in scientific research, educational activities, the European space programme and security and judicial co-operation. However, without a rebate arrangement, we may need to contribute more towards these programmes in order to do so.

Contributions to EU running costs should reduce, although we may instead need to contribute to the European Economic Area (EEA), the European Free Trade Area (EFTA) or potentially to a new UK-EU trade organisation. However, any savings are likely to be more than offset by taking back responsibilities currently run by the EU without benefiting from its economies of scale.

This leaves the main area of discussion to be about the UK's contribution to regional and social development spending in poorer EU countries, principally in eastern Europe where the UK has been a key proponent of EU expansion and NATO membership.

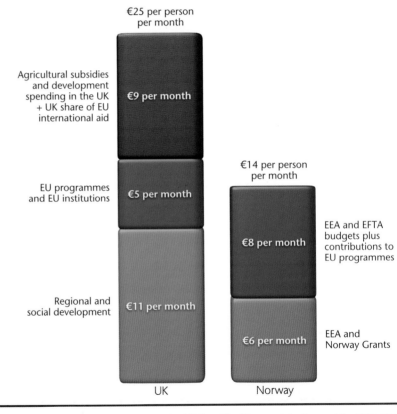

€25 per person per month

Agricultural subsidies and development spending in the UK + UK share of EU international aid — €9 per month

EU programmes and EU institutions — €5 per month

Regional and social development — €11 per month

UK

€14 per person per month

EEA and EFTA budgets plus contributions to EU programmes — €8 per month

EEA and Norway Grants — €6 per month

Norway

Total Norway contributions of €0.5bn to the EEA and EFTA budgets or in direct contributions to the EU, and €0.4bn on EEA and Norway grants, based on a population of 5.3m people.

Whole of Government Accounts

What are the Whole of Government Accounts?

Accounting as known to the world of finance

Up until this point most of the numbers presented have been based on the government's reporting of public sector finances under National Accounts rules. These are generally consistent with the way other governments around the world report their finances too.

However, it may be surprising to learn that it is only recently that governments have started to consider using similar systems of accounting to those that they have legislated for everyone else to follow. This is quite a change as government accounting is very different from the more comprehensive systems of financial accounting used by companies and most other organisations.

The good news is that the UK Government is one of the leading nations in this movement and has now published its sixth set of financial statements prepared in accordance with *International Financial Reporting Standards (IFRS)*. It describes them as Whole of Government Accounts as they include all levels of government, including local authorities.

The bad news is that these numbers show that the UK public sector's financial health is much worse than that presented in the National Accounts. This is principally because the government's traditional accounting does not reflect costs incurred that will be settled in the longer-term, such as the pensions of public sector employees or the costs of nuclear decommissioning.

The other bad news is that it takes the government more than a year to prepare the Whole of Government Accounts and so the numbers are not as up to date as they could be.

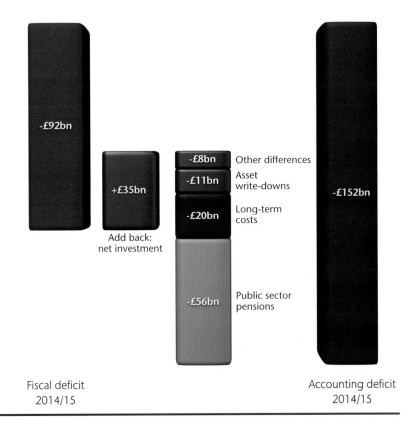

Accounting deficits are larger than fiscal deficits

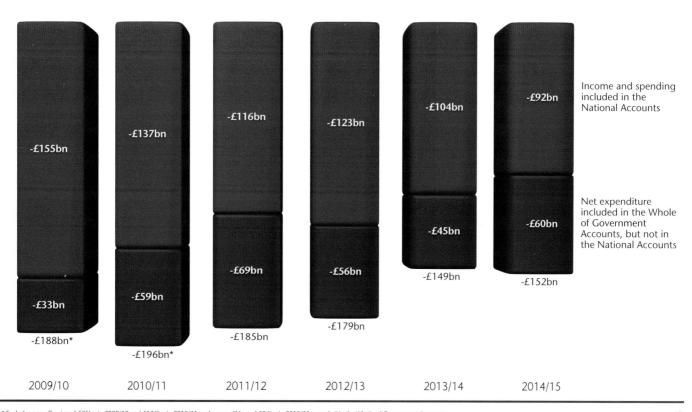

Income and spending included in the National Accounts

Net expenditure included in the Whole of Government Accounts, but not in the National Accounts

-£155bn

-£137bn

-£116bn

-£123bn

-£104bn

-£92bn

-£33bn

-£59bn

-£69bn

-£56bn

-£45bn

-£60bn

-£188bn*

-£196bn*

-£185bn

-£179bn

-£149bn

-£152bn

2009/10   2010/11   2011/12   2012/13   2013/14   2014/15

* Excludes one-off gains of £25bn in 2009/10 and £126bn in 2010/11 and a one-off loss of £24bn in 2010/11 recorded in the Whole of Government Accounts.

What is in the balance sheet?

Assets of £1.5tn and liabilities of £3.6tn

The balance sheet sets out the government's financial position - what it owns and what it owes.

At 31 March 2015, assets recorded in the balance sheet amounted to £1.5tn (£23,000 per person). This included infrastructure such as roads, railways, schools, hospitals and public housing, together with offices, other property, plant & equipment, receivables, investments and financial assets.

Assets were more than offset by liabilities of £3.6bn (£55,000 per person). These are much higher than the £1.5tn in debt reported at 31 March 2015, because of sizeable obligations to pay for public sector pensions and other long-term liabilities that are not captured by government accounting.

Overall, net liabilities were £2.1tn at 31 March 2015, approximately £32,000 for each person living in the UK.

It is important to understand that the values placed on assets do not necessarily represent the amounts that could be realised if they were sold. Infrastructure assets, for example, are valued at how much they would cost to rebuild and not at their market value. In practice, most assets could not be sold in any case as they are required to deliver public services or to support the economy.

Furthermore, not all future political promises or commitments are recorded as liabilities. In particular, the balance sheet does not capture political commitments to continue paying the state pension or other welfare benefits into the future.

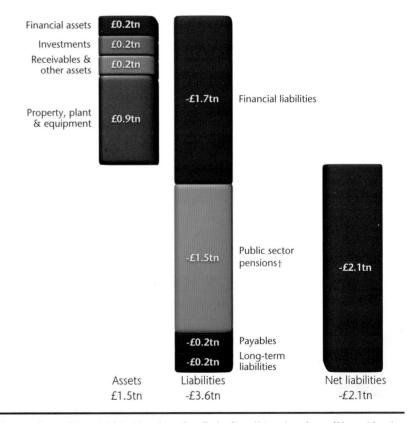

Financial assets £0.2tn

Investments £0.2tn

Receivables & other assets £0.2tn

Property, plant & equipment £0.9tn

-£1.7tn Financial liabilities

-£1.5tn Public sector pensions†

-£0.2tn Payables

-£0.2tn Long-term liabilities

-£2.1tn

Assets £1.5tn

Liabilities -£3.6tn

Net liabilities -£2.1tn

† This relates to accumulated pension entitlements of public sector employees, and does not include the state pension or other welfare benefits payable to pensioners. See page 50 for more information.

Key balances at 31 March 2015

Financial assets £180bn		
Bank deposits and short-term loans	£79bn
Foreign reserves	£57bn
Cash	£27bn
IMF special drawing rights	£9bn
Gold holdings	£8bn

Financial liabilities -£1,529bn		
Treasury bills	-£65bn
National Savings & Investments	-£124bn
Bank of England owed to depositors	-£355bn
Gilts owed to external investors	-£985bn

Financial investments £220bn		
Loans to banks and other businesses	£63bn
Student loans	£48bn
Equity investments in RBS and Lloyds Bank	£44bn
IMF and other international institutions	£20bn
Other equity investments	£20bn
Other investments	£25bn

Other financial liabilities -£188bn		
Other financial liabilities	-£3bn
Due to IMF for special drawing rights	-£9bn
Financial derivatives and guarantees	-£18bn
Banknotes in circulation	-£64bn
Bank loans and other debt	-£94bn

Receivables and other assets £207bn		
Taxes yet to be collected	£110bn
Other receivables	£36bn
Software and development assets	£32bn
Investment property & assets held for sale	£18bn
Inventories	£11bn

Public sector pensions -£1,493bn		
Funded pensions net liability	-£120bn
Unfunded pensions liability	-£1,373bn

Other property, plant & equipment £511bn		
Buildings	£231bn
Housing	£97bn
Land	£51bn
Military equipment	£32bn
Other fixed assets and equipment	£100bn

Payables -£173bn		
Tax and duty refunds due	-£27bn
PFI and finance lease liabilities*	-£43bn
Payable to suppliers and others	-£48bn
Accruals for costs and deferred income	-£55bn

Infrastructure assets £337bn		
Highways	£112bn
Local authority roads	£62bn
Network Rail	£54bn
Transport for London	£32bn
Other infrastructure assets	£77bn

Long-term liabilities -£175bn		
Potential tax refunds	-£15bn
Pension protection schemes	-£24bn
Other exposures	-£24bn
Clinical negligence claims	-£29bn
Nuclear decommissioning costs	-£83bn

* Total obligations under PFI and other lease contracts amounted to £230bn, of which £109bn related to future services, £59bn in future interest and £19bn to future payments on operating leases.

How will we pay for public sector pensions?

Net pension obligations of £1.5tn at 31 March 2015

Central government policy is to not set aside money for public sector pensions.

As a consequence, government departments, schools, police forces, fire services and the armed forces pay for the pensions of their retired employees out of their current budgets. Contributions from current employees are not invested and instead go towards paying the pensions of previous generations of employees.

This contrasts with local authorities and some other public bodies (such as the BBC and the Bank of England) that have taken a different route and established pension funds into which both employer and employee contributions are invested, setting aside money now to pay out in the future.

The £1.75tn total obligation (before deducting investments) is discounted, meaning that it is less than the total future payments that will need to be made. It is calculated by working out how much would need to be put into 'low risk' financial investments to cover those payments once income on those investments is taken into account. As interest rates are very low, the discounted value of the obligation is closer to the total amount of payments due than would be the case if expected investment returns were higher.

Generally, most pension funds invest in equities and other investments with higher returns and so in practice establishing funds for central government pension schemes would require less than the £1.37tn value for the obligations presented in the Whole of Government Accounts.

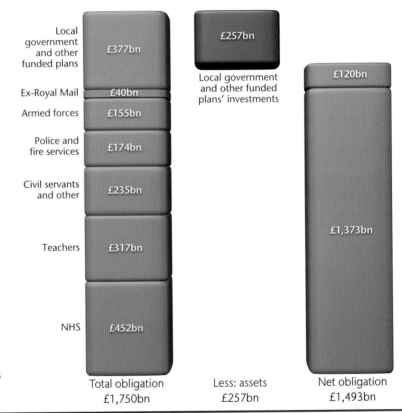

Local government and other funded plans £377bn
Ex-Royal Mail £40bn
Armed forces £155bn
Police and fire services £174bn
Civil servants and other £235bn
Teachers £317bn
NHS £452bn

Total obligation £1,750bn

£257bn
Local government and other funded plans' investments

Less: assets £257bn

£120bn
£1,373bn

Net obligation £1,493bn

* Pension liabilities shown are for the pension entitlements of current and former public sector employees. They do not include state or war pensions, which are recorded in the year they are payable.

Economy & population

How big is the economy?

Over £1.9tn of transactions each year in the UK

The principal benchmark used to measure the size of the UK economy is Gross Domestic Product (GDP). This is despite GDP being a very rough estimate of economic activity that is frequently revised.

GDP represents the value of transactions generated within the UK economy. As one person's income is another person's spending, it can be calculated either by adding up how much people and businesses earn, or alternatively by adding up how much everyone spends, as shown on pages 54 and 55.

GDP is expected to add up to £1,943bn this year, an average economic activity of £2,470 per person per month.

This is based on a forecast for the economy to grow by 1.8% after inflation, comprising 0.8% from population growth and 1.0% from an increase in the level of average economic activity per person.

Overall this means that total GDP is expected to be 3.4% higher than last year, once inflation is also taken into account.

The expected inflation of 1.5% is based on a measure known as the 'GDP deflator', which is an average of inflation rates across the whole economy. It is not the same as measures that use prices that mainly affect consumers, such as the retail prices index (RPI) or the consumer prices index (CPI), which are expected to increase this year by 1.7% and 0.6% respectively.

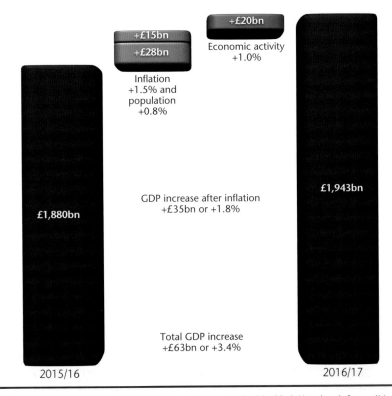

+£20bn

Economic activity
+1.0%

+£15bn

+£28bn

Inflation
+1.5% and
population
+0.8%

GDP increase after inflation
+£35bn or +1.8%

£1,943bn

£1,880bn

Total GDP increase
+£63bn or +3.4%

2015/16

2016/17

The 1.8% forecast for economic growth may turn out to be significantly different, particularly in light of the decision to leave the European Union.

Annual change in economic activity over the last decade

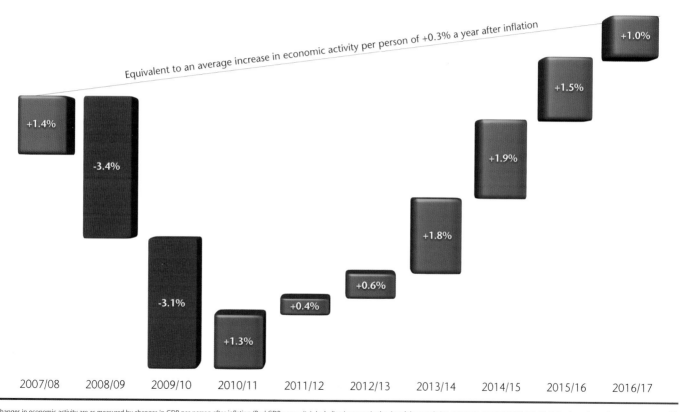

Equivalent to an average increase in economic activity per person of +0.3% a year after inflation

+1.4%
-3.4%
-3.1%
+1.3%
+0.4%
+0.6%
+1.8%
+1.9%
+1.5%
+1.0%

2007/08   2008/09   2009/10   2010/11   2011/12   2012/13   2013/14   2014/15   2015/16   2016/17

Changes in economic activity are as measured by changes in GDP per person after inflation (Real GDP per capita). Including increases in the size of the population, economic growth is 0.7% or 0.8% higher for each year shown.

What makes up GDP of £1,943bn?

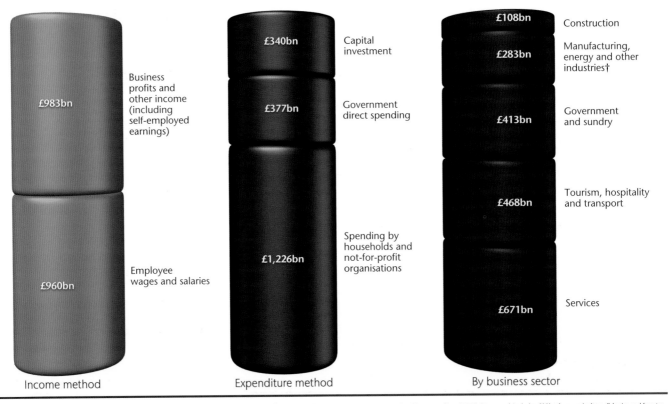

Income method

£983bn — Business profits and other income (including self-employed earnings)

£960bn — Employee wages and salaries

Expenditure method

£340bn — Capital investment

£377bn — Government direct spending

£1,226bn — Spending by households and not-for-profit organisations

By business sector

£108bn — Construction

£283bn — Manufacturing, energy and other industries†

£413bn — Government and sundry

£468bn — Tourism, hospitality and transport

£671bn — Services

Amounts extrapolated from provisional 2015 data.   † Includes £11bn from agriculture, fisheries and forestry.

GDP of £2,470 per person per month

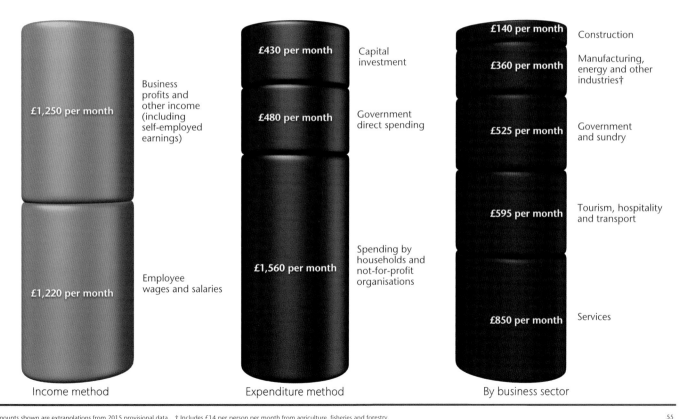

Income method

£1,250 per month — Business profits and other income (including self-employed earnings)

£1,220 per month — Employee wages and salaries

Expenditure method

£430 per month — Capital investment

£480 per month — Government direct spending

£1,560 per month — Spending by households and not-for-profit organisations

By business sector

£140 per month — Construction

£360 per month — Manufacturing, energy and other industries†

£525 per month — Government and sundry

£595 per month — Tourism, hospitality and transport

£850 per month — Services

Amounts shown are extrapolations from 2015 provisional data.   † Includes £14 per person per month from agriculture, fisheries and forestry.

55

The economy over the last decade

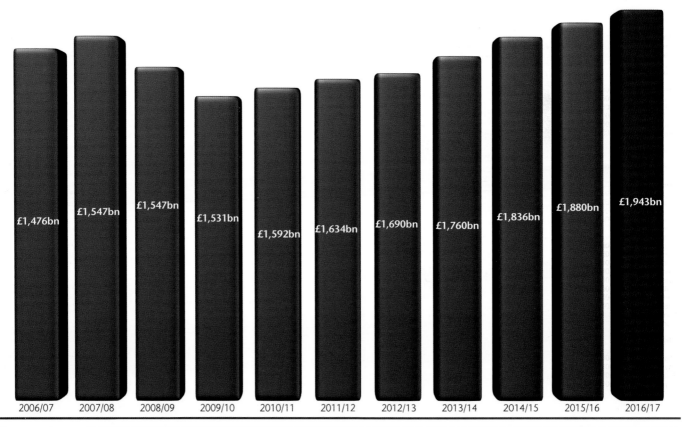

£1,476bn — 2006/07
£1,547bn — 2007/08
£1,547bn — 2008/09
£1,531bn — 2009/10
£1,592bn — 2010/11
£1,634bn — 2011/12
£1,690bn — 2012/13
£1,760bn — 2013/14
£1,836bn — 2014/15
£1,880bn — 2015/16
£1,943bn — 2016/17

The chart shows GDP for each financial year. The heights of the bars have been scaled for inflation and population growth in order to better illustrate the effect of the economic downturn and subsequent recovery.

How do we compare with the world economy of £57tn in 2016?

North America

USA	£14,100bn
Canada	£1,170bn
Mexico	£780bn

South America

Brazil	£1,470bn
Argentina	£350bn
Columbia	£210bn
Chile	£190bn
Peru	£140bn
Venezuela	£140bn

Europe

Germany	£2,640bn
UK	£1,920bn
France	£1,870bn
Italy	£1,410bn
Spain	£940bn
Netherlands	£580bn
Switzerland	£500bn
Sweden	£390bn
Poland	£360bn
Belgium	£350bn
Austria	£290bn
Norway	£280bn
Denmark	£230bn
Ireland	£190bn
Finland	£180bn
Portugal	£160bn
Greece	£150bn
Romania	£140bn
Hungary	£100bn

Africa

Nigeria	£250bn
Egypt	£230bn
South Africa	£230bn
Algeria	£120bn

Middle East

Turkey	£580bn
Saudi Arabia	£470bn
Iran	£310bn
Israel	£290bn
UAE	£250bn
Qatar	£130bn
Iraq	£110bn

Eurasia

Russia	£970bn
Kazhakstan	£90bn

East Asia

China	£8,590bn
Japan	£3,740bn
South Korea	£1,090bn
Taiwan	£400bn

South Asia

India	£1,730bn
Pakistan	£210bn
Bangladesh	£180bn

South East Asia

Indonesia	£730bn
Thailand	£310bn
Malaysia	£240bn
Singapore	£230bn
Philippines	£230bn
Vietnam	£150bn

Pacific

Australia	£970bn
New Zealand	£140bn

North America £16.1tn

Eurasia £1.3tn

UK £1.9tn

East Asia £13.8tn

Europe including UK £13.2tn

Central America and Caribbean £0.3tn

South America £2.7tn

South Asia £2.2tn

Middle East £2.4tn

Africa £1.6tn

South East Asia £2.0tn

Pacific £1.1tn

Source: IMF World Economic Outlook Database 2016 - GDP by country, converted at 31 July 2016 exchange rates: £1.00 = US$1.32 = €1.18 = CNY 8.79 = JPY 135 = INR 88 = BRL 2.70 = CAD 1.72 = KRW 1.86 = RUB 87 = AUD 1.74

57

What is the balance of payments?

A current account deficit of £82bn

In theory, the balance of payments comprises two equal and opposite elements for flows coming into and leaving the country: the 'current account' and the financial or 'investment account'.

In practice the estimated amounts for these items do not balance exactly, as the statisticians are not able to track every transaction in the economy and instead use samples and estimates of varying quality.

The current account deficit is broken into three components: the earnings deficit from salaries, profits and investment income generated in the UK transferred abroad net of transfers the other way, the trade deficit from imports and exports, and other receipts and payments, including international aid and contributions to the EU and other international organisations.

At the time of the 2016 Budget, the expectation was that the current account deficit would be £82bn (4.2% of GDP) this year, a reduction compared with the then estimated current account deficit last year of £96bn (5.1% of GDP).

The surplus on the investment account this year was expected be around £80bn, comprising inward investment in the order of £150bn less outward investment of around £70bn.

A note of caution. Forecasts of the current account deficit and the investment surplus are highly likely to be wrong, as international trade and financial flows are subject to many different economic factors that can change rapidly.

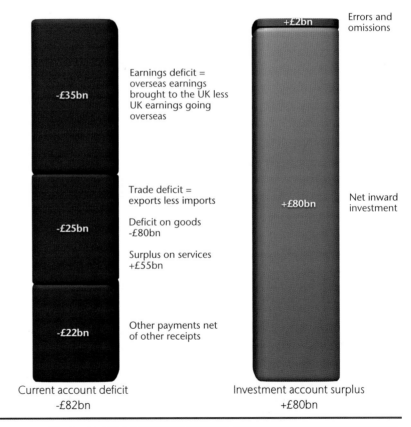

-£35bn — Earnings deficit = overseas earnings brought to the UK less UK earnings going overseas

-£25bn — Trade deficit = exports less imports

Deficit on goods -£80bn

Surplus on services +£55bn

-£22bn — Other payments net of other receipts

Current account deficit -£82bn

+£2bn — Errors and omissions

+£80bn — Net inward investment

Investment account surplus +£80bn

* Based on extrapolations from 2015 provisional economic data. Actual amounts for 2016/17 could be significantly different.

Who do we import from and export to?

Europe	Imports	Exports
Germany	£71bn	£24bn
France	£38bn	£33bn
Netherlands	£37bn	£30bn
Spain	£25bn	£15bn
Belgium	£23bn	£16bn
Ireland	£18bn	£27bn
Italy	£20bn	£17bn
Switzerland	£12bn	£20bn
Norway	£14bn	£6bn
Sweden	£10bn	£8bn
Poland	£10bn	£6bn
Denmark	£5bn	£6bn
Portugal	£5bn	£3bn
Austria	£4bn	£3bn
Finland	£3bn	£3bn
Greece	£3bn	£2bn
Romania	£2bn	£2bn
Hungary	£3bn	£2bn
Luxembourg	£2bn	£2bn
Baltic states	£2bn	£1bn
Malta	£1bn	£1bn

Americas	Imports	Exports
USA	£61bn	£104bn
Canada	£8bn	£7bn
Mexico	£2bn	£2bn
Brazil	£2bn	£4bn
Argentina	£1bn	£1bn
Chile	£1bn	£1bn
Columbia	£1bn	£1bn

UK dependencies	Imports	Exports
Jersey	£5bn	£5bn
Guernsey	£2bn	£4bn
Gibraltar	-	£3bn
Isle of Man	£1bn	£1bn
Cayman Islands	-	£1bn
British Virgin Islands	-	£1bn
Bermuda	-	£1bn

Africa, Middle East and Eurasia	Imports	Exports
South Africa	£4bn	£4bn
Nigeria	£2bn	£2bn
Egypt	£1bn	£2bn
Algeria	£2bn	
Morocco	£1bn	£1bn
Angola	£1bn	£1bn
Turkey	£9bn	£5bn
UAE	£4bn	£9bn
Saudi Arabia	£2bn	£7bn
Qatar	£3bn	£3bn
Israel	£2bn	£2bn
Kuwait	£1bn	£1bn
Iraq	-	£1bn
Oman	-	£1bn
Russia	£5bn	£6bn
Kazakhstan	£1bn	£1bn
Azerbaijan	-	£1bn

Asia-Pacific	Imports	Exports
China	£48bn	£25bn
Japan	£10bn	£11bn
South Korea	£5bn	£6bn
Taiwan	£4bn	£2bn
India	£10bn	£7bn
Pakistan	£2bn	£1bn
Bangladesh	£2bn	-
Sri Lanka	£1bn	-
Singapore	£4bn	£8bn
Thailand	£4bn	£2bn
Vietnam	£4bn	£1bn
Malaysia	£2bn	£2bn
Indonesia	£1bn	£1bn
Philippines	£1bn	£1bn
Cambodia	£1bn	-
Australia	£5bn	£9bn
New Zealand	£1bn	£1bn

Imports £555bn

- Europe: £320bn
- Americas: £80bn
- Asia-Pacific: £105bn
- Africa, Middle East and Eurasia: £40bn
- UK dependencies: £10bn

Exports £530bn

- Europe: £260bn
- Americas: £120bn
- Asia-Pacific: £80bn
- Africa, Middle East and Eurasia: £55bn
- UK dependencies: £15bn

Amounts shown are extrapolations from 2015 provisional data and are rounded to the nearest billion pounds. Regions have been rounded to the nearest £5bn.

Measures for the size of the economy

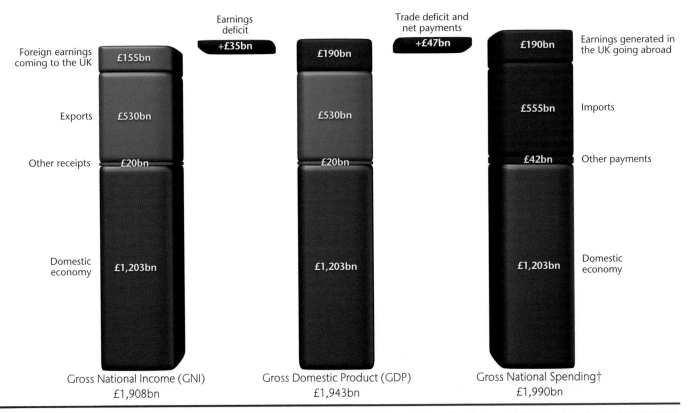

Earnings deficit +£35bn

Trade deficit and net payments +£47bn

Foreign earnings coming to the UK £155bn

Exports £530bn

Other receipts £20bn

Domestic economy £1,203bn

£190bn

£530bn

£20bn

£1,203bn

Earnings generated in the UK going abroad £190bn

Imports £555bn

Other payments £42bn

Domestic economy £1,203bn

Gross National Income (GNI) £1,908bn

Gross Domestic Product (GDP) £1,943bn

Gross National Spending† £1,990bn

Amounts shown are extrapolations from 2015 provisional data. † Gross National Spending is not an official statistic and is shown to illustrate how the current account deficit relates to GDP.

How much are we worth?

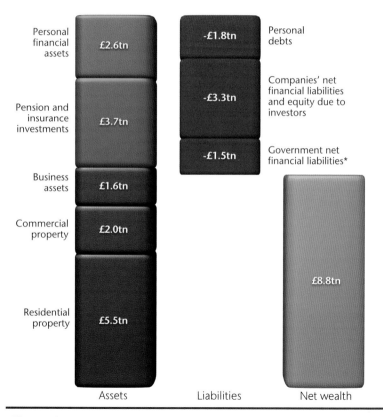

Personal financial assets — £2.6tn

Pension and insurance investments — £3.7tn

Business assets — £1.6tn

Commercial property — £2.0tn

Residential property — £5.5tn

Personal debts — -£1.8tn

Companies' net financial liabilities and equity due to investors — -£3.3tn

Government net financial liabilities* — -£1.5tn

Net wealth — £8.8tn

Assets   Liabilities   Net wealth

Average wealth of £135,000 per person

The net value of UK assets was estimated by the Office for National Statistics to be £8.8tn at the end of 2015, or around £135,000 per person living in the UK at that time. Of course in reality a few people are worth a lot more than this, while the majority have much less.

The largest element of the UK's wealth is in property, with homes worth £5.5tn and commercial properties of £2.0tn. Business assets comprise machinery & equipment of £0.9tn, inventories of £0.5tn and intellectual property of £0.2tn.

Personal financial assets and investments were valued at £6.3bn, before taking account of £1.8tn in personal debts.

Government financial assets of £0.7tn were less than its £2.2tn in liabilities*, while companies' financial assets of £22.4tn were more than offset by £25.7tn in financial liabilities and equity due to investors.

£40,000
£57,000
£24,000
£30,000
£85,000

-£28,000
-£50,000
-£23,000

£135,000

Average assets and liabilities per person

* This estimate of government liabilities is on a different basis to the £3.6tn (£55,000 per person) in the Government's latest financial accounts as shown as page 48.

61

How many of us are there?

There are 65.8m people living in the UK

The population of the UK is expected to comprise 65.8m people at 30 September 2016, the mid-point of the government's financial year.

Approximately 55.6m people, or 84% of the population, live in England, with a total of 10.2m people (16%) living in Scotland, Wales and Northern Ireland.

Within England, just over half live in the South and East (28.8m), a fifth in the Midlands (11.5m) and just over a quarter in the North (15.3m).

There are 32.5m males and 33.3m females, making up 49.4% and 50.6% of the population respectively, or around 102 females to every 100 males.

The median age is 40, with half of the population under the age of 40 and the other half over 40, as shown in more detail on page 64.

We live in 27.4m households, of which 7.9m are single person households, 9.6m comprise two people, 4.4m have three people and 5.5m have four or more people. Of the households with more than one person, 18.6m are family households and 0.9m are with unrelated adults sharing.

Around 48m of the population are currently registered to vote, of which an estimated 1.5m are eligible to vote in local elections and 46.5m are eligible to vote in both national and local elections (and referendums).

Scotland
5.3m

North East
2.6m

Yorkshire
5.5m

East Midlands
4.8m

East Anglia
4.4m

Greater London
8.8m

South East Coast
5.6m

Home Counties
5.4m

South West
4.6m

Greater Birmingham
2.8m

Mercia
3.9m

Wales
3.1m

Greater Manchester
2.9m

North West
4.3m

Northern Ireland
1.8m

*England does not have official states or provinces and is instead split into smaller city-regions, counties and unitary authority for administrative purposes.

How is the population increasing?

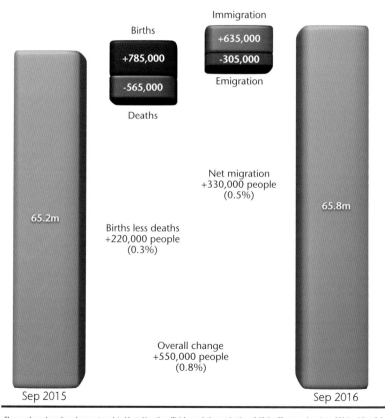

Births
+785,000
-565,000
Deaths

Immigration
+635,000
-305,000
Emigration

65.2m

65.8m

Net migration
+330,000 people
(0.5%)

Births less deaths
+220,000 people
(0.3%)

Overall change
+550,000 people
(0.8%)

Sep 2015

Sep 2016

An increase of 0.8% in population this year

The population is estimated to have increased by 550,000 people over the course of the year to September 2016, a growth rate of 0.8%.

This rate of increase is significantly higher than the average increase of 0.6% a year in the UK's population over the last twenty years, during which it has increased from 58.2m in 1996 to 65.8m in 2016 as shown on page 64.

Natural changes (births less deaths) contributed around 220,000 of the increase this year, with a relatively low death rate as people live longer.

Around 5,000 of the deaths each year are of those under the age of twenty, 10,000 are in the 20-40 age range, 50,000 in the 40-60 age range, 200,000 are aged between 60 and 80 and 300,000 are over 80. These represent annual mortality of 0.03%, 0.06%, 0.3%, 1.6%, and 9.4% for each age group respectively.

Net migration is roughly 330,000 and comprises an estimated increase of 180,000 EU citizens (270,000 arrivals less 90,000 departures) and 190,000 non-EU citizens (280,000 arrivals less 90,000 departing), offset by a decrease of approximately 40,000 in British citizens (125,000 leaving the UK less 85,000 returning).

Of the immigrants arriving each year, around 305,000 come to work, 165,000 arrive to study, 80,000 come to join family and 45,000 are claiming asylum, with the other 40,000 coming to the UK for other reasons.

The numbers above have been extrapolated by taking the official population projection of 65.6 million people at June 2016, adding 0.1m for higher than projected net migration and 0.1m to adjust from June to September.

63

How much older are we getting?

We are living longer

The number of people living in the UK has increased by 7.6m over the last twenty years to reach 65.8m. There have been 15.5m births, 11.8m deaths and net migration of 3.9m in that time.

Living longer is the main reason for this increase. The number of people over the age of 40 has increased by 6.6m out of the total increase in the population of 7.6m. As a consequence the median age of the population has increased to 40 years old, up from 37 in 1996.

Without migration, the number of people under the age of 40 would have declined by approximately 1.9m, instead of the 1.0m increase that has actually occurred.

This is a 3% increase over the last 20 years, compared with a 25% increase in the number of people over the age of 40 in the same period (of which 4% is from net migration).

Over the next twenty years the population is expected to grow by a further 7.6m people, with a projected 16.0m births, 12.1m deaths and net migration of 3.7m, with a projected median age in 2036 of 43. Alternative scenarios range from 69m to 77m people living in the UK in 2036.

Financial projections for the next twenty years are on the basis of net migration continuing to contribute around 0.2m people a year to the working age population. If net migration is reduced below this level, there could be less tax revenue available to pay for the pensions, health and social care of older people.

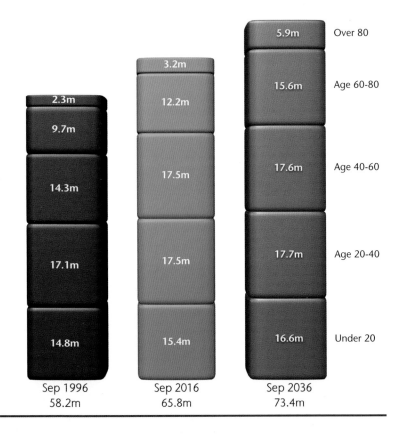

What do we all do?

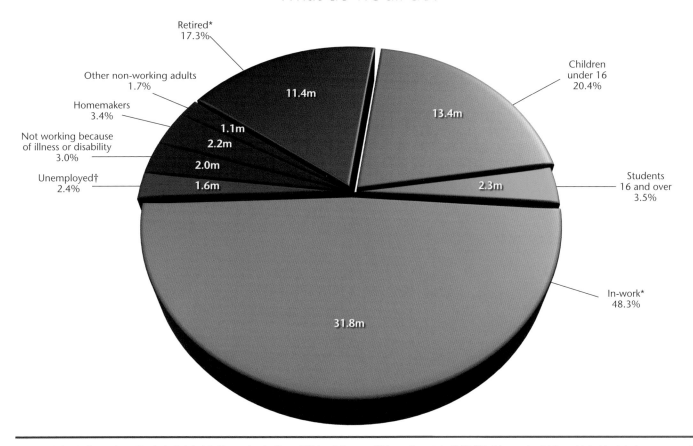

Retired*
17.3%

11.4m

Other non-working adults
1.7%

Homemakers
3.4%

1.1m

2.2m

Not working because
of illness or disability
3.0%

2.0m

Unemployed†
2.4%

1.6m

Children
under 16
20.4%

13.4m

Students
16 and over
3.5%

2.3m

In-work*
48.3%

31.8m

---

* In-work includes 1.2 million people over 65 and retired includes 1.2 million people under 65.   † This is equivalent to an official unemployment rate of 4.9%. Of the 1.6m unemployed, 0.7m are claiming jobseeker's allowance.

A world population of 7.3bn people

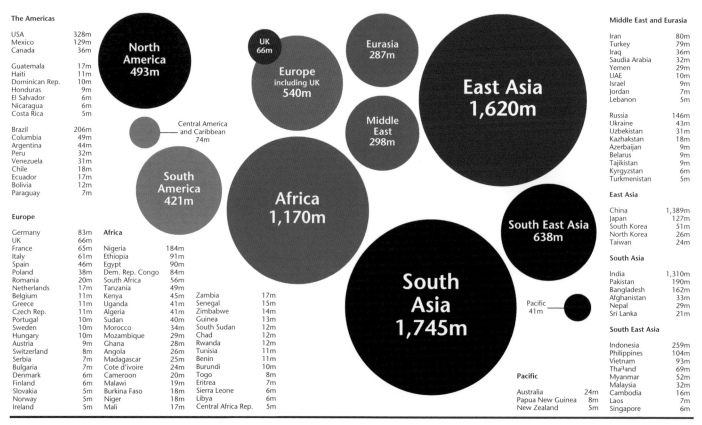

The Americas

USA	328m
Mexico	129m
Canada	36m
Guatemala	17m
Haiti	11m
Dominican Rep.	10m
Honduras	9m
El Salvador	6m
Nicaragua	6m
Costa Rica	5m
Brazil	206m
Columbia	49m
Argentina	44m
Peru	32m
Venezuela	31m
Chile	18m
Ecuador	17m
Bolivia	12m
Paraguay	7m

Europe

Germany	83m
UK	66m
France	65m
Italy	61m
Spain	46m
Poland	38m
Romania	20m
Netherlands	17m
Belgium	11m
Greece	11m
Czech Rep.	11m
Portugal	10m
Sweden	10m
Hungary	10m
Austria	9m
Switzerland	8m
Serbia	7m
Bulgaria	7m
Denmark	6m
Finland	6m
Slovakia	5m
Norway	5m
Ireland	5m

Africa

Nigeria	184m		
Ethiopia	91m		
Egypt	90m		
Dem. Rep. Congo	84m		
South Africa	56m		
Tanzania	49m		
Kenya	45m	Zambia	17m
Uganda	41m	Senegal	15m
Algeria	41m	Zimbabwe	14m
Sudan	40m	Guinea	13m
Morocco	34m	South Sudan	12m
Mozambique	29m	Chad	12m
Ghana	28m	Rwanda	12m
Angola	26m	Tunisia	11m
Madagascar	25m	Benin	11m
Cote d'ivoire	24m	Burundi	10m
Cameroon	20m	Togo	8m
Malawi	19m	Eritrea	7m
Burkina Faso	18m	Sierra Leone	6m
Niger	18m	Libya	6m
Mali	17m	Central Africa Rep.	5m

Pacific

Australia	24m
Papua New Guinea	8m
New Zealand	5m

North America 493m

UK 66m

Europe including UK 540m

Eurasia 287m

East Asia 1,620m

Central America and Caribbean 74m

South America 421m

Africa 1,170m

Middle East 298m

South East Asia 638m

South Asia 1,745m

Pacific 41m

Middle East and Eurasia

Iran	80m
Turkey	79m
Iraq	36m
Saudia Arabia	32m
Yemen	29m
UAE	10m
Israel	9m
Jordan	7m
Lebanon	5m
Russia	146m
Ukraine	43m
Uzbekistan	31m
Kazakhstan	18m
Azerbaijan	9m
Belarus	9m
Tajikistan	9m
Kyrgyzstan	6m
Turkmenistan	5m

East Asia

China	1,389m
Japan	127m
South Korea	51m
North Korea	26m
Taiwan	24m

South Asia

India	1,310m
Pakistan	190m
Bangladesh	162m
Afghanistan	33m
Nepal	29m
Sri Lanka	21m

South East Asia

Indonesia	259m
Philippines	104m
Vietnam	93m
Thailand	69m
Myanmar	52m
Malaysia	32m
Cambodia	16m
Laos	7m
Singapore	6m

Source: IMF World Economic Outlook Database April 2016 - population estimates for 2016 for countries with 5m people or more, rounded to the nearest million people.

Taxes & welfare

Personal taxes

The British tax system is extremely complicated

There are three different taxes on personal income, incorporating seven different tax bands at different levels of earnings, or nine bands if you have children.

This is before taking into account the complexities of the tax treatment of interest and dividends or the bewildering array of allowances and deductions that may also apply. Or the way capital gains are treated, with those lucky enough to own their own homes able to bank potentially very large gains tax-free, while those owning a second home or a property they rent out have to pay a higher rate than they would on other forms of investment.

There is also the use of a set of different tax rules for those individuals running their own businesses directly as sole traders or in partnerships, as opposed to those running their businesses through limited companies.

Nevertheless the following pages represent an attempt to summarise the tax and welfare system operating in the UK.

They illustrate the absurdities of a system designed to be progressive, but which frequently fails to achieve that aim, particularly when combined with welfare benefits as described on pages 72 and 73.

Despite all its flaws the personal tax system does achieve its principal objective of collecting a significant amount of money for the government, with £316bn this year expected to be generated by income tax, national insurance and capital gains tax, some 44% of total taxes and other income.

Income tax and national insurance

Income tax is paid on annual earnings above £11,000 at rates of 20%, 40%, 60%, 40% or 45% at different levels of income, with an extra rate for those with children. In addition, employee national insurance is payable at a rate of 12% of annual salaries between £8,060 and £43,000 a year and 2% of salaries above that.

Employer national insurance

Employers' national insurance is a payroll tax paid by employers at a rate of 13.8% on annual salaries above £8,060.

Dividends and interest

Dividends up to £5,000 are tax-free, while interest of £500, £1,000 or £5,000 is tax-free, based on total earnings.*

Interest - above threshold	20% or higher
Dividends - above £5,000	7.5%
Dividends - higher rate taxpayer	32.5%
Dividends - top rate taxpayer	38.1%
Individual Savings Account (ISA)	0%

Capital gains tax

Capital gains tax of 20% is due on total gains in excess of £11,100, with a lower 10% rate if total income including gains is less than £54,000. There are exemptions for a primary home, car and for personal possessions sold for less than £6,000. There is an extra 8% due on sales of second homes and residential property investments.

Allowances

The main allowance is the personal allowance, which shelters the first £11,000 of earnings.

Personal allowance	£11,000
Transferable to spouse†	£1,100
Married (age 81+)	+£3,220-£8,355
Blind persons allowance	+£2,290

* The first £500, £1,000 or £5,000 is tax-free for those earning over £43,000, £17,000-£43,000 and under £17,000 respectively (including the interest).   † Limited to spouses earning less than £43,000.

Up to nine different tax bands for personal income

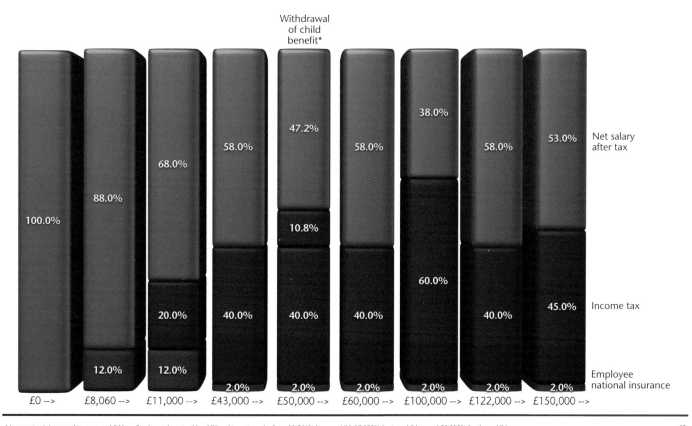

Withdrawal of child benefit*

Net salary after tax

Income tax

Employee national insurance

| £0 --> | £8,060 --> | £11,000 --> | £43,000 --> | £50,000 --> | £60,000 --> | £100,000 --> | £122,000 --> | £150,000 --> |

100.0% / 88.0% / 68.0% / 58.0% / 47.2% / 58.0% / 38.0% / 58.0% / 53.0%

20.0% / 10.8%

12.0% / 12.0% / 40.0% / 40.0% / 40.0% / 60.0% / 40.0% / 45.0%

2.0% / 2.0% / 2.0% / 2.0% / 2.0% / 2.0%

* Income tax is increased to recover child benefit where relevant - this additional tax rate varies from 10.764% for one child, 17.888% for two children and 25.012% for three children.

Transaction taxes

Transaction taxes generate a lot of money

Transaction taxes are a very effective way of collecting additional revenue. VAT alone generates almost one fifth of the total tax take; if it was abolished and replaced by higher income taxes, then income tax rates would have to be at least 66% higher.

In theory, VAT is straightforward as a tax, with most items charged at underlying sales price plus 20%. However, there are many complexities in the detail, for example in the distinction between products that attract VAT versus those that are subject to a reduced rate, zero rated or exempt.

Excise duties on fuel, alcohol and tobacco have a dual purpose in that they are designed to influence behaviour as well as raise money, although many people appear to be able to resist these influences given that these taxes continue to raise billions in pounds each year.

Alcohol duties vary by type of product and only some duties increase with alcoholic strength. For example a pint of cider attracts a fixed amount of duty of 27p as long it is less than 7.5% alcohol, compared with how the 50p duty on a pint of 4% beer will increase to 75p on a pint of 6% beer.

Stamp duty on properties is a transaction tax on sales of residential properties in England, Wales and Northern Ireland. In Scotland, there is a separate but similar land and buildings transaction tax with its own bands: 0% on the first £145,000, 2% on the next £250,000, 5% to £325,000, 10% to £750,000 and 12% over £750,000. For the purchase of second homes anywhere in the UK there is an additional 3% payable on the entire value of the property.

VAT

VAT is added to the price of most goods and services, with a reduced rate and zero rate for certain items.

Standard rate	20%
Reduced rate	5%
(e.g. domestic electricity and gas)	
Zero rate	0%
(e.g. food, children's clothes, books)	

Fuel duties

Fuel duty is levied on most fuel products. Amounts shown here include 20% VAT.

Petrol and diesel	69.5p per litre
Light oil	81.2p per litre
Aviation gasoline	45.2p per litre
Red diesel / kerosene	13.4p per litre
Fuel oil	12.8p per litre

Alcohol duties

Duties vary based on type of drink and alcoholic strength. Amounts shown here include 20% VAT.

Spirits	66p per 50ml (40%*)
Beer	50p per pint (4%*)
Strong beer	65p per half pint (8%*)
Cider	27p or 40p per pint†
Wine	£2.50 per 0.75l bottle‡
Sparkling wine	£3.20 per 0.75l bottle‡

Tobacco duties

Tobacco duties are charged on all tobacco products. Amounts shown here include 20% VAT.

Cigarettes	19.8% of retail price + 23.6p per cigarette
Cigars	£2.94 per 10g
Handrolling tobacco	£2.38 per 10g
Chewing tobacco	£1.29 per 10g

Stamp duty on properties

Purchases of residential properties are taxed with rates applying to each part of the purchase price.

First £125,000 of purchase price	0%
£125,000 - £250,000	2%
£250,000 - £925,000	5%
£925,000 - £1.5 million	10%
£1.5 million +	12%

F* Duties on spirits, beer (2.8%-7.5%) and strong beer (7.5%+) prorate by alcohol level.   † For cider (<7.5%) or strong cider (7.5%-8.5%).   ‡ For 5.5%-15% wine and >8.5% sparkling wine.

Business & other taxes

| Corporation tax | Corporation tax applies to companies, based on their taxable profits in the UK. | Standard rate | 20% |
| | | Oil and gas companies rate | 30% |

Business rates	Business rates are based on official rental values, with discounts for small businesses.	England	49.7%
		Wales	48.6%
		Scotland	51.0%
		Northern Ireland	51.7% to 59.6%

Council tax — Council tax applies to residential properties and varies by local authority, based on property bands.

England* average £94 per month x 1.36 x

Band A	0.67	Band E	1.22
Band B	0.78	Band F	1.44
Band C	0.89	Band G	1.67
Band D	1.00	Band H	2.00

Inheritance tax	Inheritance tax applies to the estates of the deceased and to gifts transferred up to seven years before.	Up to £325,000 (individuals)	0%
		Up to £650,000 (couples)	0%
		Tax on transfers to spouse	0%
		Tax on legacies to charities	0%
		Tax on assets above limit	40%
		Rate if leaving 10%+ to charity	36%

Other taxes and charges	Other government revenues include an assortment of fees, taxes and duties.	Air passenger short-haul	£13 or £26
		Air passenger long-haul	£73 or £146
		Vehicle excise duty	£0 - £515 per year
		BBC licence fee	£145.50 per year
		Passport	£72.50 for ten years

There are many other taxes and charges too

Businesses are generally subject to corporation tax, although individuals operating their own businesses as sole traders or through partnerships may be subject to income tax instead.

The standard rate of corporation tax has been reducing over the last few decades, from 35% in 1988 to 20% currently, although allowances and extra tax deductions can enable some companies to pay tax at a rate much lower than 20% of their profits. The government plans to reduce the rate further to 18% in 2017/18 and to 17% in 2019/20.

Businesses also have to pay payroll taxes in the form of employers' national insurance as described on page 68. For business owners taking profits as salary instead of as dividends, the 13.8% rate payable is equivalent to a tax of 12.1% on corporate profits.

Many businesses also pay business rates, a tax on properties and infrastructure used for commercial purposes. Rates are calculated based on official rental valuations carried out every five years or so.

Council tax applies to residential property, varying by local authority and a price band based on 1991 property values. The average household charge in England is £94 per month, although it can range from as low as £38 per month up to £293 per month depending on location and band. Council tax also applies in Scotland and Wales, while Northern Ireland uses a domestic version of business rates.

Inheritance tax applies to legacies and on gifts transferred up to seven years before death.

* Scotland average per household of £83 per month x 1.16 x band ratio. Wales average of £97 per month x 1.14 x band ratio. NI domestic rates range between 0.70% to 0.84% of rental value.

71

Welfare

The welfare system is very complicated too

The welfare system is sometimes described as operating from 'cradle to grave' by providing support through all stages of life. From benefits and tax breaks for children and their parents, through unemployment benefits, tax credits and housing support during working life, to pensions and benefits in retirement.

There is an overall cap on benefits of £1,517 per month for single people living alone and £2,167 per month for families with children, although this cap does not apply to the severely disabled or to war widows.

Child benefit until recently was given to all families, but is now reclaimed through the tax system where one or other parent earns over £50,000 a year.

Parents on low earnings may be able to receive additional child tax credits and help with up to 70% of their childcare costs.

The state pension is £502 per month (£115.95 a week) for those with 30 years of national insurance contributions. Pension tax credits provide support to those not entitled to the full pension or with insufficient other income.

Pensioner households can also receive a winter fuel payment £200 (£300 for over 80s) to help with heating costs and cold weather payments (£25 for each seven day period below zero celsius).

Out-of-work benefits

The main benefits for the unemployed are jobseeker's allowance and housing benefit.*

Jobseekers' allowance / income support
couple (per person)	£249 per month
single aged 25 or more	£317 per month
single aged 24 or less	£251 per month
Housing benefit	£195-£1,812 per month

Child benefit

Parents of children receive child benefit, but is reclaimed from parents earning over £50,000.

Child benefit
for eldest child	£90 per month
for other children	£59 per month

Incapacity & disability benefits

Support to those with disabilities depends on the level of disability. The employment & support allowance (ESA) is for those in work.

PIP living	£239 per month
PIP living severe	+£118 per month
PIP mobility	£94 per month
PIP mobility severe	+£155 per month
ESA work support	+£442 per month
Carer's allowance	£269 per month

In-work benefits

Several benefits are aimed at supporting the low paid. The rules are complicated and there are steep withdrawal rates.

Working tax credit	£163 per month
Lone parent credit	+£168 per month
Child credit per child	to £232 per month
extra for first child	+£45 per month
Childcare per child	to £455 per month
extra for first child	+£76 per month
Housing benefit*	£195-£1,812 per month

State pensions

Eligibility for the state pension is based on national insurance contributions, but pension tax credits can make up the difference.

State pension	up to £502 per month
Pension credits	up to £655 per month
Winter fuel payment	£200 or £300
Cold weather payments	£25
Bus pass	Free local travel

* Housing benefit is based on household size and location, from £195 for a single-person room in Sunderland to £1,812 for a four bedroom home in central London.

The poverty trap

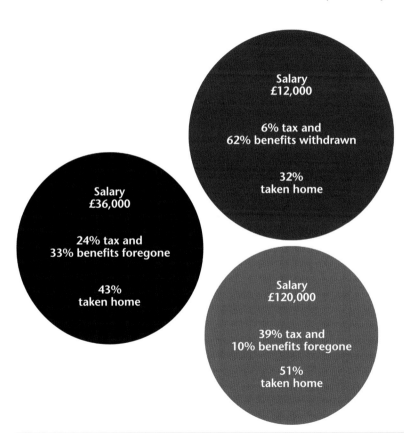

Salary £12,000

6% tax and 62% benefits withdrawn

32% taken home

Salary £36,000

24% tax and 33% benefits foregone

43% taken home

Salary £120,000

39% tax and 10% benefits foregone

51% taken home

Universal Credit is only a small improvement

The welfare system as currently designed results in the low paid losing a much higher proportion of their income to benefit withdrawal and taxes than those earning more. In some circumstances this can even mean losing money when taking a job, especially once travel and childcare costs are taken into account.

The government is in the process of trying to improve this by rolling out Universal Credit, which allows more money to be retained before benefit withdrawal starts and less penal withdrawal rates than before.

Even with Universal Credit, however, benefit withdrawal rates for the low paid are significantly higher than the top rates of income tax for those on the highest salaries or those in high earning households. This is illustrated on page 74, showing how those on benefits may end up retaining as little as 13p out of an additional pound of earnings, which compares with the 53p of each extra pound earned retained by the highest paid.

Another way of understanding this is to compare two individuals who each get a part-time job paying £1,000 a month (£12,000 a year). In an illustrative example, a single person on benefits might get to take home around 32% of their new earnings after benefit withdrawal and taxes are taken away, keeping less than one-third of their new salary.

This compares with how a wealthier second earner would be able take home between 53% and 94% of that new salary depending on their and their family's overall financial situation.

This is an illustrative example for a single person over 25 and makes assumptions around how much he or she would receive in benefits under Universal Credit and Council Tax Support at different levels of income.

73

Benefit withdrawal rates (illustrative example)

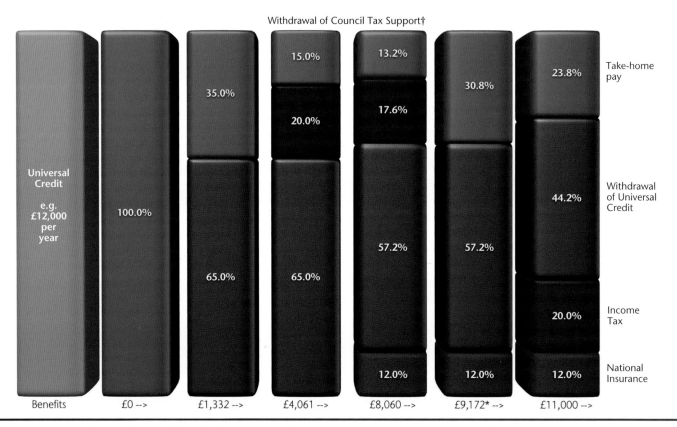

Withdrawal of Council Tax Support†

| | | | | 15.0% | 13.2% | | 23.8% | Take-home pay |

Universal Credit

e.g. £12,000 per year

100.0%   35.0%   20.0%   17.6%   30.8%

65.0%   65.0%   57.2%   57.2%   44.2%   Withdrawal of Universal Credit

20.0%   Income Tax

12.0%   12.0%   12.0%   National Insurance

Benefits   £0 -->   £1,332 -->   £4,061 -->   £8,060 -->   £9,172* -->   £11,000 -->

Illustrative examples is for a single person on £317 a month in jobseeker's allowance, £600 in housing benefit and £83 in Council Tax Support.   † The withdrawal rate for Council Tax Support can be higher in some areas.

Technical

Terminology

Why can't people just use plain English?

Unfortunately, it is not possible to publish a book on the public finances without using some technical terms.

After all, it would be difficult to discuss the economy without referring to GDP, the headline measure used by economists to estimate the size of the economy.

In some cases technical terms are hidden in plain sight. For example, debt is an ordinary English word, but when used in the context of the public finances it is actually shorthand for a defined measure that includes some financial obligations and excludes others.

The use of the word deficit is particularly challenging as in ordinary English it can refer to a cumulative shortfall as well as to a shortfall over a period of time such as a year. In the public finances the latter sense is used, which can cause confusion for people familiar with its use in other contexts, such as with a pension deficit that refers to the cumulative shortfall in a pension scheme.

Wherever possible, the same measures are used throughout the guide. GDP always means nominal GDP, inflation is always the GDP deflator, and an increase in economic activity always means an increase in Real GDP per capita.

Unfortunately, the term deficit varies depending on the context. In the main it refers to the fiscal deficit, the primary measure used by the government. Other meanings have been prefixed to clarify that a different definition is being used, as with *accounting* deficit, the *structural* deficit or the *current account* deficit.

Size of the economy

GDP or Gross Domestic Product refers to nominal GDP or GDP at market values, with the effect of inflation shown explicitly between years. This differs from the use of GDP at current values, which involves changing numbers to eliminate inflation between years.

Inflation

Inflation has been calculated using the average measure used for the entire economy, known as the *GDP deflator*. This differs from other measures such as the consumer prices index (CPI) or the retail prices index (RPI).

Change in economic activity

A change in economic activity means an increase or decrease in nominal GDP after adjusting for both inflation and population growth. This is equivalent to a change in GDP per person after inflation, officially *Real GDP per capita*.

Deficit

The deficit (or fiscal deficit) is equal to *public sector net borrowing* in the National Accounts (*current receipts* less *total managed expenditure*). The accounting deficit refers to *revenue less expenditure* in the Whole of Government Accounts, while the current account deficit relates to the balance of payments for the economy.

Debt

Debt is the National Accounts measure *public sector net debt excluding nationalised banks*, also referred to as *PSNDex*.

Sources

Budget 2016

The income and expenditure amounts for 2016/17 used in this guide are primarily based on the 2016 Budget 'Red Book' forecasts issued in March 2016 by HM Treasury and the related Economic and Fiscal Outlook report published by the Office for Budget Responsibility (OBR) at the same time.

PESA 2016

The annual Public Expenditure Statistical Analyses (PESA) published by the Office for National Statistics provided another source of information, together with other financial updates provided by HM Treasury and the OBR, including the OBR Public Finances Databank.

National Accounts

Additional information on the economy has been derived from the National Accounts 'Blue Book', published in October 2015, together with other more recent economic data from the Office for National Statistics, which has been extrapolated to form the basis for analyses of the economy.

National Population Projections

Information on the UK population has been primarily based on the official population estimates and projections published by the Office for National Statistics.

Other sources

Other significant sources include HM Revenue & Customs, central government departments, the Scottish, Welsh and Northern Irish administrations, the European Commission, the International Monetary Fund and some local authorities.

Official numbers, with some adjustments

The numbers included in this guide are primarily based on official financial information and statistics published by HM Treasury, the Office for National Statistics and the Office for Budget Responsibility, as well as from the European Commission and the International Monetary Fund.

In order to improve comparability and to minimise the number of different periods presented, adjustments have been made to get to the numbers published in this guide.

For example, the official projection for the population at 30 June 2016 of 65.6m has been extrapolated to get to the estimate of 65.8m at 30 September 2016, reflecting higher net migration numbers than originally projected as well adjusting for a difference of one calendar quarter.

There were some particular frustrations as a consequence of the classification of spending in the Budget issued by HM Treasury being different to that used to report public expenditure by the Office for National Statistics. This meant that some guesswork was required to complete certain analyses, such as the more detailed spending breakdowns on pages 19 and 21.

The government continually updates financial information and official statistics and so the numbers presented in this guide may not be up to date. It also frequently changes the way it defines income and spending, so that amounts may not always be comparable between different financial periods.

Actual versus budget for 2015/16

If only we could accurately forecast the economy!

One thing that often confuses people about government finances is that the numbers can move around, sometimes by very large amounts.

Part of this is normal for any organisation - a budget at the start of the year is updated with forecasts during the year, followed at the end of the year with a final report providing the financial results actually achieved. The government is more susceptible to variability because it deals with the long-term and forecasts income and spending many years ahead of time. With more opportunity for policies and circumstances to change the likelihood of forecasts being accurate is that much lower.

Further confusion is caused by frequent changes in the way government does its accounting. Over the last few years, changes have been to include Network Rail as part of the public sector (from 2014 onwards), the discovery in 2015 that housing associations had been incorrectly omitted from the numbers since 2008, and the adoption of new UN and EU rules in 2014.

To illustrate these changes it is useful to compare the deficit for 2015/16. It was expected to be £75bn when forecast in the 2015 Spring Budget, but four months later the 2015 Summer Budget had reduced that to £69bn, with a better economic forecast as well as additional tax rises and spending cuts. Since then the government has brought housing associations into the National Accounts, while taxes and other income came in £2bn less than the June 2015 Budget expectation and spending ended up £2bn higher.

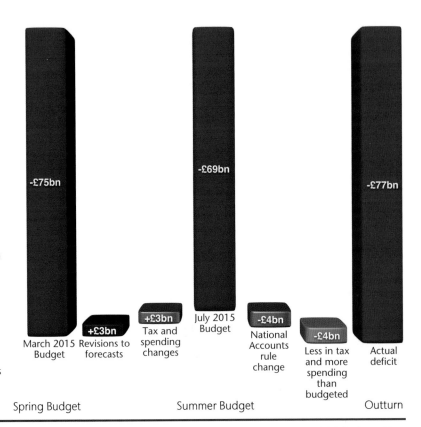

-£75bn — March 2015 Budget
+£3bn — Revisions to forecasts
+£3bn — Tax and spending changes
-£69bn — July 2015 Budget
-£4bn — National Accounts rule change
-£4bn — Less in tax and more spending than budgeted
-£77bn — Actual deficit

Spring Budget   Summer Budget   Outturn

2015 Spring Budget taxes and other income of £667bn less spending of £742bn. 2015 Summer Budget £673bn less £742bn. Actual deficit (subject to audit) £678bn less £755bn, inc £7bn and £11bn respectively for housing associations.

What are DEL and AME?

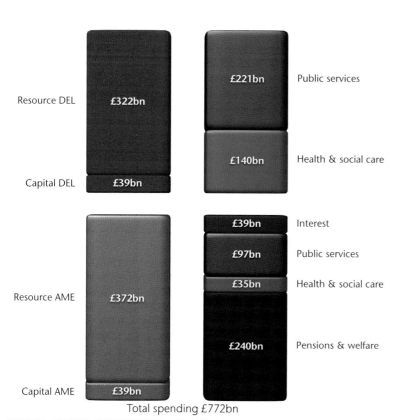

Resource DEL — £322bn

Capital DEL — £39bn

£221bn — Public services

£140bn — Health & social care

Resource AME — £372bn

Capital AME — £39bn

£39bn — Interest

£97bn — Public services

£35bn — Health & social care

£240bn — Pensions & welfare

Total spending £772bn

Department expenditure limits (DEL) and annually managed expenditure (AME)

One of the more confusing aspects of government accounting is the classification of spending between DEL and AME.

Ostensibly this is supposed to help with budgeting by differentiating between the multi-year spending budgets allocated to departments and more variable spending that can change each year due to demand or circumstances.

Unfortunately, adding a fourth dimension to the standard three dimensional budgeting approach (who is responsible for the spending, what the money is being spent on, and why it is being spent) makes it particularly difficult to follow what is going on.

This is compounded by the significant differences between the numbers used for budgeting purposes, the numbers in the National Accounts for statistical reporting purposes and the numbers used in the Whole of Government Accounts under International Financial Reporting Standards. This involves accounting differences in the tens of billions of pounds between different views of the spending budget.

As a consequence there is very little understanding of how the public finance numbers fit together, even by those responsible for managing those finances.

Holding the government to account for its financial performance is therefore much more difficult than it needs to be.

The split of health and social care and public services between DEL and AME is illustrative only as it is based on some guesstimation.

Debt as a share of GDP

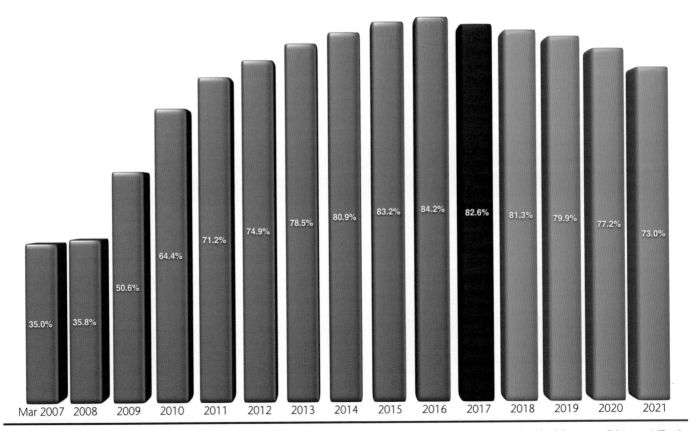

Mar 2007	35.0%
2008	35.8%
2009	50.6%
2010	64.4%
2011	71.2%
2012	74.9%
2013	78.5%
2014	80.9%
2015	83.2%
2016	84.2%
2017	82.6%
2018	81.3%
2019	79.9%
2020	77.2%
2021	73.0%

Based on debt at the end of the financial year divided by mid-year GDP (i.e. GDP for the second half of the previous financial year and the first half of the subsequent financial year). Future years are likely to turn out differently.

2014/15 Whole of Government Accounts as a share of GDP

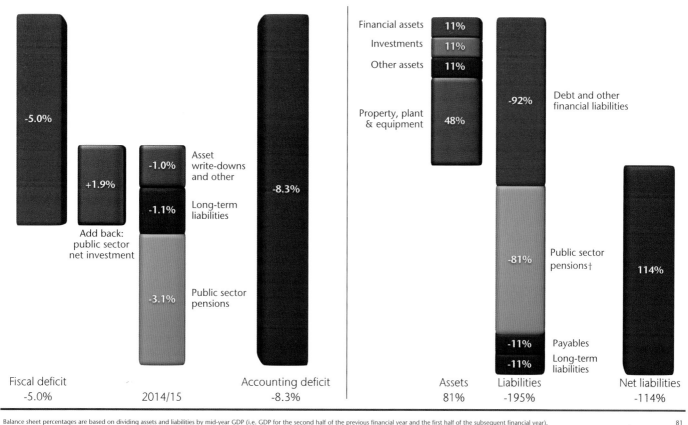

2016/17 taxes and other income of 36.9% of GDP

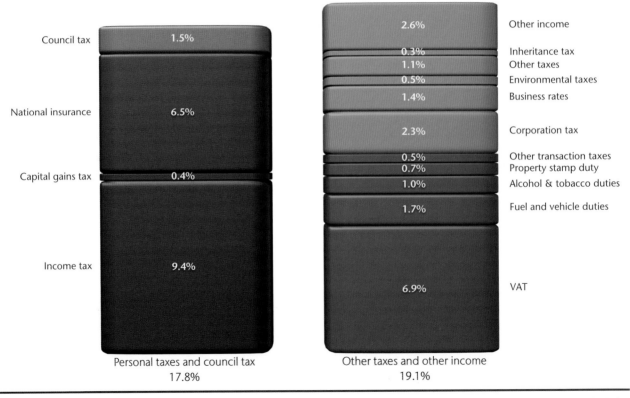

Council tax — 1.5%

National insurance — 6.5%

Capital gains tax — 0.4%

Income tax — 9.4%

Personal taxes and council tax
17.8%

2.6% — Other income
0.3% — Inheritance tax
1.1% — Other taxes
0.5% — Environmental taxes
1.4% — Business rates
2.3% — Corporation tax
0.5% — Other transaction taxes
0.7% — Property stamp duty
1.0% — Alcohol & tobacco duties
1.7% — Fuel and vehicle duties
6.9% — VAT

Other taxes and other income
19.1%

Based on budgeted taxes and other income for 2016/17 of £716n and expected GDP of £1,943bn.

2016/17 spending of 39.8% of GDP

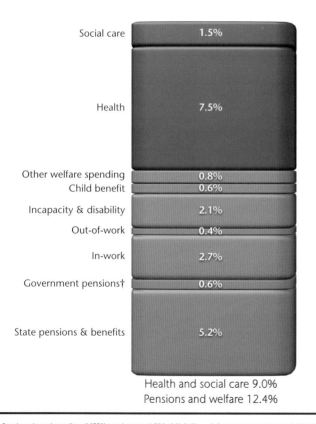

Social care — 1.5%

Health — 7.5%

Other welfare spending — 0.8%
Child benefit — 0.6%

Incapacity & disability — 2.1%

Out-of-work — 0.4%

In-work — 2.7%

Government pensions† — 0.6%

State pensions & benefits — 5.2%

Health and social care 9.0%
Pensions and welfare 12.4%

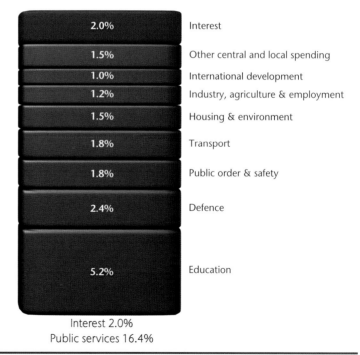

2.0% — Interest

1.5% — Other central and local spending

1.0% — International development

1.2% — Industry, agriculture & employment

1.5% — Housing & environment

1.8% — Transport

1.8% — Public order & safety

2.4% — Defence

5.2% — Education

Interest 2.0%
Public services 16.4%

2016/17 tax and spending as a share of GDP

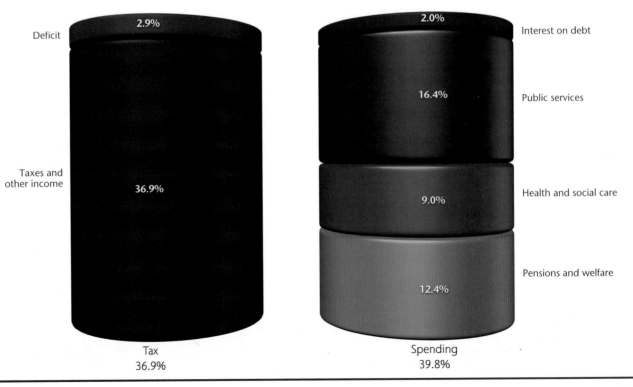

Deficit — 2.9%

Taxes and other income — 36.9%

Interest on debt — 2.0%

Public services — 16.4%

Health and social care — 9.0%

Pensions and welfare — 12.4%

Tax
36.9%

Spending
39.8%

Percentages shown are based on the 2016 Summer Budget. Actual income and spending may turn out to be different, as may GDP.